PRAISE FOR FEMI...

"*Feminist to Feminine* is a timely guide for women of all ages who are feeling dissatisfied in their lives trying to implement modern-day feminism. This book is a brilliant resource for any woman searching for her true God-given identity, and provides practical advice about careers, relationships, and reproduction. Kuehl offers an alternative: lean into your femininity and embrace God's unique calling to women to "mother" the world around. *Feminist to Feminine* is a must-read for women everywhere."

—MONIQUE ISRINGHAUSEN, Miss Florida USA 2020

"Hopeful, realistic, personal. Justice is wonderfully vulnerable, depicting the struggle between the church and the Feminist world beautifully. As a communicator, she has a unique understanding of femininity by way of the tragic and ever-present contradiction of being a "modern-day woman." In a world so dominated by notions of defiant Feminism, a sense of true, real, biblical femininity has been overlooked for too long. Justice's personal journey into motherhood has only heightened her intellectual and philosophical understanding of femininity and the rottenness of modern-day Feminism. This book establishes a woman's true source of power and allows the reader to feel warmed by the message and takeaways. Every young woman should read this work and ponder the journaling prompts with an urgent seriousness and desire for reflection. I absolutely recommend this to any age woman, in any stage of life!"

—LILY KATE, CEO OF VICTORY, Public Speaker

"*Feminist to Feminine* was an awakening and thought-provoking to what being Feminine truly means. Reading this book was an invitation to take a deeper look into my own life and the modern definition of a feminist. As I read, I realized that I needed to disentangle my belief in what being a feminist means. My identity isn't in a "movement," but it is rooted in who created me and the gifts God has given me. I was liberated to be feminine. I would encourage every woman to read this book."

—ELLISON FOWLER, Wife + Mother

"If you've ever had questions about feminism or femininity, this is the book for you. Justice discusses the pitfalls of feminism with compassion and discernment, opening my eyes to aspects of the history of feminism that I was unaware of. Justice gives insight on the gift of femininity and how God created women for a unique purpose. This book helped nurture my femininity through understanding the spiritual and physical gifts God has given to us as women. The best part of this book is learning about Justice's own Christian testimony and journey in femininity. I am so grateful for her vulnerability and honesty in sharing her journey from feminist to feminine and learning how God worked in her life. In a world that views femininity as a weakness, rather than a strength, this book is an excellent guide filled with Biblical truth for navigating who God calls us to be as women."

—CATARINA GARZA, Doctor of Pharmacy Graduate Student

Reclaiming the Value of
Womanhood in God's Story

FEMINIST
TO
FEMININE

Justice Hope Kuehl

Fedd Books
P.O. Box 341973
Austin, TX 78734

www.thefeddagency.com

Cover art by Marlita Gonzales
Cover design by Mackenna Cotten

Published in association with The Fedd Agency, Inc., a literary agency.

ISBN: 9781957616513
eISBN: 9781957616520

LCCN: 2023918935

Printed in the United States of America

TABLE OF CONTENTS

FOREWORD

I've lived long enough to know that what I've struggled with as a female, especially in my early years, is quite common for most of us girls—a fear of the lack of control over the constant changes in our bodies, a longing to be nurtured and accepted by the women in our lives, a yearning to be adored and cherished by the men in our lives, and a fierce ache to accomplish truly meaningful things. These core drivers find a unique expression in each of us and, at some point or another, we can end up back in the fetal position, sorting through all our related pain and insecurities. For years I felt exhausted with my own complicatedness and enraged at the idea of anyone else thinking that about me. Yet, I've avoided relationships with other girls or women who felt complicated to me. I craved simplicity but had no idea it was rooted in the issues that my own daughter dares to untangle in her heart and in the book you are about to journey through.

I would like to be able to tell you that the truths about feminism Justice has discovered and written about in these pages came as an overflow of her mom—me—investing them into her with thoughtful intention because I had the feminist vs feminism debate all clear in my own heart. But I did not. As Justice's mother, I can only say that I'm thankful she landed in such a healthy place after her very personal and unique pursuit. Even with the profound love I have for my four daughters (and son), my role as a woman in society was something I stumbled into at best.

Because my own mom died young, I was fueled by a passion to make sure that my life mattered—and the sooner the better because you never know. I loved being a mother and raising daughters (we adopted our son later in life). I was often seriously overwhelmed because, while I was fully invested in my role as wife and mother, I was also fully panicked at the thought of not getting to be everything I thought I could be. I was desperate to matter in every way. For me, that meant having an impact through ministry in addition to all that I was doing for our kids. Because my husband was in ministry, to him it often felt like I was just jealous of him. I knew I was proud of him and I believed I played a critical role in his ministry, but in truth I was jealous of the illusive home-run-over-the-fence kind of feeling you get from achieving success. As a mom I hadn't mastered finding joy in the small wins and nothing I accomplished was ever truly complete. I mean—dishes, diapers, and laundry don't stay finished, right?! The mundane had lied to me and I had agreed. "Being a woman is thankless, less meaningful than being a man, and holds me back from something I just can't quite grasp." I felt like a failure most days, when in reality, if I could have simply believed it, I was actually in my sweet spot for that season of my life. I mattered as much as any person ever has.

I'm certain that if I had gone on the intentional journey that you are venturing into inside of "Feminist to Feminine," I would have avoided years of striving for what God had already planned to give me in His time. My heart would've been able to celebrate where I was rather than where I could be, and my daughters would've witnessed a trust in God that's more real than all the fear-based life lessons I preached to them. I wish that was all that's at stake for you and this generation of women, but it certainly is not.

What began in the heart of the enemy of God in the garden of Eden with an assault on the first woman, continued throughout time until it found a name—the Women's Liberation Movement. What appeared to be nothing but a new level of freedom and validation for women's equality was, I believe, a shiny hook we swallowed. It has led to what we now see being played out in classrooms, sports, and laws surrounding the very definition of a woman and the watering-down of all that makes us different from the men we are trying to be validated by. The repercussions of this battle that we didn't realize we were fighting hits at the most fundamental aspects of our God-given gifts of our beauty, our ability to conceive, sustain life, birth and nurture, along with all of the other nuances of our femininity. If we are made in God's image, male and female, then in our fear and panic, are we actually coming against the One who made us? Is the enemy getting what he wanted from the beginning by playing on insecurities that can only be healed by embracing the truth that only God can provide?

Reading this book—my daughter's book—was honestly the first time I realized the full weight of my perspective, or lack of, on the issues surrounding our role as women in society. Of course, as her mom, my personal battle to understand my role as a woman was never something I was intentional about. I grieve that she was left to struggle her way through this critical subject for herself when I could have helped her and provided a more firm foundation as a female at this time in history. When we don't decide with purpose and intention what we believe and why we believe it, we fall into the agenda and trap that has been chosen by a very real enemy. The consequences are more than we can possibly know, both in our personal lives and relationships, as well as in the next generation and the very fabric of society itself.

I often tell people that I've learned way more from my children than I ever taught them. Justice, like each of them, has not only given me more opportunities to lean into God as she overcame so many hurdles in life, but also poured back into me words of wisdom she gained in her pain and processing. What a joy it is for me to know that someone who would not exist apart from all that makes me who I am as a woman, is pouring out wisdom for you as well. Who will you say that about some day? Whether you ever have natural children or not, you have the capacity within you to reproduce yourself, to birth justice for your own life-story.

I remember when I was pregnant with Justice Hope and we prayed about what to name her. As clear as you can perceive God's voice, we sensed her name was to reflect what we were learning in life at the time—God is our source and hope for justice. His justice isn't revenge, but rather His redemption and ability to make even the worst things better than if they had never happened. In essence, that is what this book is about—God taking all of the worst parts of what you have been through, bringing you through to the other side of them, and you being able to pour your victories into the lives of others. There's nothing more powerful or more beautiful.

I urge you to be intentional with this topic. Even if you disagree with some of Justice's perspectives, you and those you are called to impact deserve the time this will require. Go deep with yourself and the Lord so that you land in a place that is thoughtful and unwavering. Each of you were created to be so convinced of your value that you are able to live focused and fulfilled through each stage of life as a woman and daughter of God—confident in the roles you will uniquely fill— fully yourself, fully present, and fully alive.

—ELIZABETH ENLOW

"What's missing in our cultural myopia is the woman of Hebraic power. Oh, we have plenty of powerful women these days. But they come to us in Greek form. They exercise their strength through political compulsion or cultural attraction. We are in awe because they are goddesses from Olympus, not doers of the Word. They promote the values of the age rather than the virtues of the Lord. And there are plenty. They are not hard to find. If you are lucky, you will find an 'eshet hayil. [excellent woman]"

—SKIP MOEN

LETTER TO THE READER

Dear Sisters,

This book was written especially for you. To help you trade deep longing for fulfillment, anger for peace, and confusion for a strong sense of identity.

As women, we find ourselves torn between wanting to be seen and treated as equals with men, but also wanting to feel the freedom to be women—to embrace even the parts of ourselves that have been unappreciated by culture.

Our collective dissatisfaction with the status quo is so evident that many different women's movements have been created in the hopes of finding solutions for what plagues us. Some of those include radical feminism, gender theory, and the Tradwife movement—just to name a few. Regardless of your political leaning, you have almost certainly felt this tension. In her groundbreaking book, *The Feminine Mystique*, Betty Friedan referred to it as "the problem that has no name."

What is this tension all about? It has to do with our careers, our relationships with men, our reproductive capacity, our friendships with other women, and the very definition of what it means to be a woman. While many of us know we *should* be able to find answers in God and His Word, we don't know where to begin.

Culture, the education system, the beauty/fashion industries, and even our families are all constantly trying to tell us who we should be as women. Finding our true identity involves recognizing these messages that compete with who God says we are. We have to understand how God's Word applies to the big dilemmas we face as women. Sure, it's nice to know that God created us in His image and calls us to be His disciples, but we must discover how that truth is meant to shape us as we navigate the world of social media, choose what to wear, consider who to date, determine values to embrace, decide if and when to have children, and more. We must develop a deep desire for truth above comfort if we are to find answers to these big questions.

The disciples of Jesus had to leave behind their previous lives and become experts on Him—abandoning their ideas of religion and allowing Jesus to redefine that for them. Jesus lived in full surrender to the Father. In that same way, we must leave behind old ways of viewing the world and instead seek to view reality through the eyes of Jesus. In John 8:31–32, Jesus promises that this level of devotion to Him—leaving our agendas behind and embracing His perspectives—will enable us to know the truth and be set free!

There is an unshakable sense of peace that comes with our surrender to God and His truth. Truth brings freedom, and freedom brings peace. We won't find peace by waiting around for things to become perfect. Instead, we must recognize that we are not limited by the restraints the world has placed on us. The first of the Ten Commandments is to have no other gods before Him. This commandment is not a means to control us; rather, it is a means for bringing freedom!

When we refuse to have any other gods before Him, not feminism or any other ideology, we find infinite freedom in the feminine identity that He offers us. Granted, our lives won't be all rainbows

LETTER TO THE READER | xv

and butterflies, but in the midst of our inevitable struggles will find fulfillment beyond belief.

We're also going to explore the radicalization of women through the "feminist" movement—a movement that began as a unifying, righteous call for equal rights for women but has since become divisive, politicized, and vilifying.

But first, a little about me. I grew up in a very female family. I am one of four daughters, my dad has six sisters, my mom has two sisters who also have daughters, and even our pets were mostly female. My childhood could be perceived by many as some sort of Disney fairytale, sheltered from the brokenness of the world by the careful love of my mom and dad. I was free to thrive in my femininity from early on. Having so many sisters and female cousins gave me a deep value for sisterhood and how beautiful our female relationships can be when we meet as sisters instead of competitors.

My "claim to fame" is that I served as the longest-reigning Miss Tennessee USA in 2020. My platform was helping women get an earlier diagnosis for endometriosis after my own ten-year battle with the debilitating disease. Since giving up my crown, I have gotten married and am currently in labor with a little boy (literally right now!). I am birthing my first book and first baby in the same year!

Growing up around women fueled my desire to protect and fight for them. It also made me feel responsible for breaking down any limitations (real or perceived) placed on women.

As I competed in pageants, I was a huge defender of the feminist message. With the exception of abortion, I was almost in complete harmony with the political messaging of the modern women's movement. Smashing the patriarchy and ensuring women were equally represented in every profession became important missions for me.[1] When

---

[1] My definition of patriarchy is a culture structured around male leadership in the home and community.

I became a "successful" young woman and felt betrayed by the very movement I had championed, I quickly became disenchanted with the hypocrisy of modern feminism.[2]

My personal success felt insufficient and did not bring fulfillment to my life, so I began the journey that I hope to bring you on through this book. I started asking God the hard questions. I decided to open my heart to hearing whoever God wanted to speak through, and I stopped placing limitations on Him and the role His Word played in my life. I have since found an anchor of peace in my life that has transformed everything that I do.

I intentionally filled the pages of this book with poetry, confessions, celebrations, questions and answers, and deep thoughts about the meaning of life as a woman in the hope that the immersive experience will help you further develop the innate feminine image that God placed in you. The book is divided into sections that will connect with your heart no matter your stage of life. You'll find reading pages where I share my heart, quotes from some of the greatest minds throughout history, facts and statistics, and journaling pages. These journaling pages are meant to be our time of discussion. Some are prompted and some are dedicated to exploring your own thoughts and questions. Let these journal entries be a place of transparency and safety for you to grow.

My hope is that, through the pages of this book, you will begin to sense the ways God is using our broken world to bring redemption to your identity as a woman—that you will reconnect with the feminine heart of God and live out your divine calling to mother the world around you. Our hypocritical culture shames us for the choices we make (regarding careers, family life, how we dress, etc.), fogging

---

[2]My definition of feminism will become more clearly defined in future chapters, but essentially feminism began as a political movement intended to fight for equal protection under the law for men and women but has since become an ideological lens that all interaction between men and women is viewed through—pitting men (oppressors) against women (the oppressed).

the lens that we see ourselves through. Our Father doesn't shame us. Instead, He removes our need to prove ourselves and helps us embrace our natural callings, gifts, and skills.

Let's embark on this journey of discovering who our Father created us to be, valuing the role men play in our lives, leaning into our femininity, and becoming the women we desire to be. Let's deconstruct the feminist bounds that have tried to hold us back and embrace the freedom which we have been called into together.

Some of my favorite memories with my sisters and female cousins are of us piled up on a sofa in our pajamas, eating cookies and laughing while we catch up. That's the place I hope you can envision yourself in as you read this book. Get cozy and let your walls down. Listen, think, consider, and share your heart on these pages. We're all sisters from different walks of life and different backgrounds, but with one common purpose: to discover who God created us to be as individuals *and* as women.

I hope you know that you have a place here—a place for your story, your experiences, your pain, and the things you wrestle with. We're all so different, but that is part of what makes the bonds of sisterhood so beautiful—sisterhood is transcendent, meaning the female experience connects us regardless of our backgrounds or histories.

No matter your age or circumstances, I want you to know that I see you, boldly determined to find the answers to your own tension. I also hope that our conversations here will help you grow in compassion, love, and truth in how you relate to the other women you interact with in your daily life. We can help other women ease the tension in their hearts if we are willing to meet them with our walls down and offer them the same emotional safety we so desire.

This book is for women of every age and walk of life–those who have experienced challenges and questions about their identity, relationships, and purpose, who are seeking God for the answers. For those who have walked with God their entire life, or who are meeting Him now for the first time. Maybe you have suffered from health issues, abuse, insecurity, or the pain of a broken heart. Perhaps you are in a season of victory and simply want to think more deeply about God's purpose for you as a woman. These pages seek to acknowledge the struggles and triumphs of being a woman in a modern world and to remind your heart that we are never too late for God's plans.

We need each other—every age, every ethnicity, and every political background. As we will soon get into, the enemy has tried desperately to come at our sisterhood. He's tried to convince us to leave the path God has laid out for us, bringing pain and destruction with him. I don't know about you, but I want no part of that plan!

Thank you for being here. I pray we all end this journey together stronger than we started!

With all my heart,
Justice Kuehl

Throughout this book, you will find journaling pages with prompts. Feel free to use the prompts I have created—or not! Maybe God is highlighting something different for you specifically. Consider this book as a conversation between us rather than a monologue by me. In some sections I have also added "Deeper Dive" reflections for readers who would like to get into the nitty-gritty of the topics we'll discuss.

- As you embark on this journey, think about your hopes and expectations. What do you desire to gain or learn from reading this book? Take a moment to write down your thoughts and aspirations.

- What does prioritizing truth over comfort look like for you? Take a moment to reflect on different areas of your life where you might be choosing comfort over truth. Jot down a list of these areas and consider how you can intentionally pursue truth in each of them.

- Are there any deep longings or areas of tension within your heart that you associate with your experience as a woman? Take some time to reflect on these emotions and write about them here. Allow yourself to be honest and vulnerable in exploring your thoughts about your femininity.

SECTION I

The War on Women: Our Real Enemy

"The great danger for family life, in the midst of any society whose idols are pleasure, comfort and independence, lies in the fact that people close their hearts and become selfish."

—SAINT JOHN PAUL II

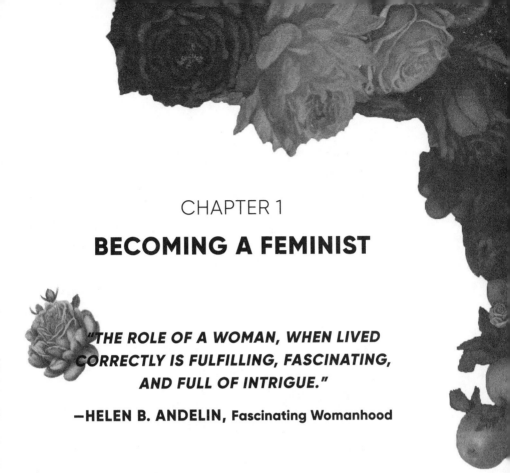

CHAPTER 1

BECOMING A FEMINIST

"THE ROLE OF A WOMAN, WHEN LIVED CORRECTLY IS FULFILLING, FASCINATING, AND FULL OF INTRIGUE."

—HELEN B. ANDELIN, Fascinating Womanhood

When I was very little, my parents started a church in our home. It quickly grew from a small gathering into a vibrant church community with a spacious church building, children's ministry, and worship team. My parents led together, both focusing on their areas of strength. My dad did most of the teaching and preaching, and my mom did much of the administrative work.

At the time, I never thought much about which tasks were "more spiritual." I was just proud of my parents and the countless ways I saw them continually putting God and His Kingdom first in our family. I was proud to be a part of what they were doing and, by extension, a part of what God was doing.

During the first few years of their church, I saw countless people come through the sanctuary (which doubled as our living room). Our times of worship together were pure and powerful. There was no choir or stained glass to help us turn our affections toward the Lord. But He met us all there. It was common for worship and prayer to go on for long stretches of time while teary-eyed visitors experienced God's presence for the first time.

As the church grew, my parents created a leadership team composed of several families who would help them pastor the expanding congregation, and the children of those families became my closest friends. We were a very tightknit group who did almost everything together. Not only did we spend Sundays together, but we were also all homeschooled together.

When I was around ten years old, my parents began considering who they should ordain as co-pastor. The natural thought was that this role would be filled by one of the husbands from the leadership team families. One Sunday, as my parents were seeking the Lord for clarity about the position, a guest speaker preached at the church. At the end of his message, he shared that he believed God wanted him to ordain my mom as the co-pastor—right then and there! My parents hadn't even considered my mom as the person for the job because it was not common for women to be pastors in the Deep South at that time.[1]

Still, my parents had no idea that commissioning my mom as co-pastor would trigger such a dramatic response from the leadership team. All but one of the couples were horrified that my mom, a woman, would now serve in a pastoral position, and they let my parents know that they completely disagreed with this decision in a less-than-honorable way. Though they apologized years later, their initial reaction was to leave the church altogether.

---

[1] This story is not meant to be a statement on whether or not women should be pastors; rather, my intention is to provide important context regarding my journey from feminism to biblical womanhood.

As a young girl, I couldn't make sense of why all of my closest friends had suddenly left our church and dissolved our community. My parents attempted to explain the nuanced theology behind the disagreement, but all my ten-year-old brain picked up on was that there are people in this world who think that men are better than women. I vowed to dedicate my life to proving those people wrong. This might seem like a dramatic reaction for a child, but with a name like Justice, I have never taken *any* perceived infringements lightly.

This experience was the first time I became aware that people might place limitations on me, my mom, and my sisters simply because we were girls. I also started recognizing that the most-praised positions in the church were largely only available to men, which troubled me. What other things did people think I could or should not do because I was a girl? And so began my new mission in life: proving that I was just as capable as any boy of taking on any challenge in the world. I felt validated by the feminist messaging that was being thrown my way and was emboldened to take my newfound passion to the extreme.

I remember telling my dad around this time that I was going to become the first woman to play professional baseball on a men's league—a rather comical idea, considering I had never even touched a baseball in my life. After a trip to Washington, DC, when I was eleven years old, I became obsessed with the idea of becoming the first female president and regularly sported a "Future President" sweatshirt while devouring books about politics. My mind was constantly plotting how I could personally break every glass ceiling. Every few months I felt a new "calling" that I was certain I was put on this earth to accomplish. My parents tried to encourage me to just be a kid, but I was propelled forward by an unbridled desire to advance the female species.

I had a friend who took violin lessons with me. He was particularly gifted (sort of a prodigy), and consequently, even though he started playing a few years after I did, he quickly surpassed my ability. This was very distressing for me. When I voiced my frustration to my parents, they told me I needed to accept that he had a natural talent that I simply did not. They were trying to help relieve me of the pressure to excel that I continually placed on myself, but I often took their advice as a challenge.

All the while, beneath my blind ambition, I still felt a deep desire to fully surrender to my femininity—to play with dolls, try on my mother's lipstick, and memorize my nana's chocolate chip cookie recipe. As I grew older, I longed to make my corner of the world more beautiful, have children, prepare for marriage, learn homemaking skills, and ditch the weight of responsibility for the destiny of all women that I felt obligated to carry on my little shoulders.

I saw the world through a black and white lens. There were two sides, good and evil. On one side was the complete subservience of women. Wives were regarded as little more than housekeepers and caregivers in the home who were expected to unconditionally obey and serve all men. I had witnessed this dynamic among many of my friends' parents. Their fathers seemed to rule their families tyrannically, and I wanted nothing to do with that.

On the other side was the complete "liberation" of women. Husbands and wives were two sides of the same coin. Women were allowed (and encouraged) to prove themselves in every area. They were expected to be mothers and doctors and play professional sports on the men's teams. It wasn't enough for women to just be happy; they were supposed to want to prove something to the world and gain motivation from that desire. Adopting this feminist perspective did little to produce any sort of real happiness in me; rather, it simply added to the insane pressure that I placed on myself as a child, and later as an adult.

JOURNALING:

- Have you ever felt the pressure to be EVERYTHING as a woman? Have you ever felt like being who you are now is not enough? Where do you think this pressure has come from?

- How did your childhood impact your view of femininity and the role of women?

MY FEMINIST YEARS

Over the years my worldview, shaped by my mother's ordination experience, primed me to accept almost every premise of feminism. I battled with my desire to function in any traditional female role and focused my energy wholly on what I considered female progress.

Feminism seemed to be a movement that represented my values. Like many other women, I called myself a feminist before I even knew what it meant. Someone probably explained to me that it was "pro-woman," and that was good enough for me. This was around the time that #thisiswhyineedfeminism was going viral. My Christian sensibilities that were disgusted by rap songs that sexually objectified women were also validated by this era of the feminist movement. Jesus and feminists were both reviled by crude language attributed to women. Jesus and feminists were both enraged by men who took sexual advantage of women. And, therefore, it seemed clear to me that Jesus and feminists were on the same page.

Not someone to stay on the fringes of a topic, I dived deeper into feminism during my college years. I started learning the history of the suffragettes and the women's liberation movement. My family had relocated from Atlanta, Georgia, to Los Angeles, California, and I enjoyed meeting so many other "open-minded" Christians. Around this time, my sister introduced me to Bernie Sanders, and although I was initially wary of his socialist agenda, I eventually became a supporter when I saw that he, too, was a feminist.

Around this same time, I was experiencing debilitating health challenges that regularly limited my mobility. I tore the cartilage in my hip and went through a series of painful injections that were supposed to heal the tear without surgical intervention. Every two weeks my mom drove me to the doctor's office on Wilshire Boulevard where I would get ten to fifteen shots in my hip joint. The pain was always so intense that I was stuck in bed for several days afterward.

Much to my disappointment, the injections didn't heal my hip joint, so I was scheduled for reparative surgery. To add insult to injury, I experienced my very first breakup a few weeks before I went under the knife. I spent my recovery time feeling pretty sorry for myself and needed something to fill my time. I sat in bed accompanied by my dog Radio, who took it upon himself to "protect" me while I recovered. We stumbled upon the social justice genre of documentaries. My heart ached as I learned about the many shocking atrocities people all over the world face. I learned all about a family in Colorado who was sick because their tap water was contaminated with natural gas, a young mom in East Asia who had to leave her daughter to live in another village while she worked for a dollar a day in a factory, and a little girl who sat by her mother's dead body in war-torn Afghanistan.

I looked down at my hip, then around at my beautiful bedroom. My soft pink sheets with little roses printed on them, the beautiful view out my window, and my sweet little dog who was cuddled up against me. My hip hurt and I couldn't walk without crutches, but maybe my circumstances weren't so bad after all.

The film *The True Cost* arguably had the biggest impact on me. I wept as I learned about the horrible living and working conditions women and girls in third world countries endure to make our fast-fashion clothes. Their exploitation and suffering broke my heart and ultimately inspired me to get my degree in fashion. I wanted to find a way to make an impact that would change the system. I wanted to educate more people on just how destructive the fast-fashion industry is while doing something to help those working in textile factories overseas.

As I laid in my soft, rosy sheets one night and slowly drifted to sleep, I was suddenly awakened by a memory—a flier I had received in the mail years earlier inviting me to compete in a local pageant. The thought had crossed my mind before, but I had never met the qualifications. Until now.

PASSIONATE TO PAGEANT GIRL

The Holy Spirit was whispering to my heart, "Now is the time!" I sat up in bed, realizing this could be the platform God wanted me to use to help make the world a better place. I fumbled around in the dark for my phone and opened a note-taking app. "I can compete in a pageant," I typed.

When I woke up the next morning, the reality of those words hit me, and I started second-guessing myself. "I'm not *really* going to do this. I'm not a pageant girl." But still, the Holy Spirit kept nudging me until I finally signed up for the Miss Los Angeles County pageant, a local preliminary for the Miss America pageant. Having absolutely no idea what I was doing, I went to YouTube for help.

At the pageant, a fellow contestant taught me how to tease my hair. Another explained the amazing benefits of a spray tan (she was right!). Every woman I met there was genuinely kind to me, the newbie. I was instantly hooked. Although I failed to capture the title of Miss Los Angeles County, I succeeded in meeting other women who wanted to change the world! In the past, I had been sneered at when

I shared my big dreams of shattering glass ceilings and changing the world with God, but the women at the pageant were already shattering glass ceilings. I decided pageants were the best vehicle for working toward my big goals, and I felt God inviting me on an adventure with Him through the process.

Pageants allowed me to gain a platform of influence while also indulging my feminine desires to dress beautifully and carry myself with grace and poise. I spent the next three years tirelessly working to excel academically while developing my outer beauty in the hope of becoming Miss California USA. I served as the vice president of my university's honors association. My GPA was among the top 5 percent at my university, and I was nominated for an academic award. My pageant career was looking up as I began placing higher each year at the state pageant (not a small feat, as California was regularly seeing 130 contestants in my category each year).

THE PERIOD FROM HELL

During these years of college and pageants, my health took another turn for the worse. My hip had finally healed, but the random abdominal pain I had experienced in high school became more severe. Eventually, I found myself in the emergency room, certain that my appendix was rupturing. I was in more pain than I thought a human could bear, but the doctors couldn't figure out its source. Sent home with a bottle of pain pills and ultrasound findings of "free fluid in the abdomen," I crossed my fingers and hoped my problems would somehow resolve themselves with a diet change.

When I realized the pain was associated with my period, I used the little information I had gained in the hospital to diagnose myself with endometriosis—a bleak prognosis with no known cure. To make matters worse, I learned that endometriosis often causes infertility. This was something my twenty-three-year-old brain hadn't planned on having to consider.

My life continued to be interrupted by rupturing cysts and excruciating abdominal and pelvic pain. I found it ironic that our cycles are called periods, because mine felt more like several exclamation points demanding more attention each month. I was desperately asking God for a miracle, for a glimmer of hope that my life would not be defined by this disease.

He answered in the form of a specialist surgeon who, upon meeting me and reviewing my case, told me prophetically, "This will not be your life, and you will be a mother." He performed a life-changing seven-and-a-half-hour surgery when I was twenty-four, and upon recovering, I've never dealt with the debilitating symptoms of endometriosis again.[2]

This experience had a profound impact on my life and further heightened my resolve. My mission to become Miss California USA became even more important, and I recognized the significance serving in a position like that would bring to my life and the lives of the millions of other women who feel limited by endometriosis.

RECLAIMING FEMINISM

The eight months following my surgery were some of the darkest days of my life. Coming off a three-month course of opioids, recovering from major abdominal surgery, learning to live with a few less inches of intestine, and faced with far too much time to think, I found myself questioning everything. Having recently graduated college, I had

---

[2]If you think you might be suffering from endometriosis, Dr. Andrew Cook at Vital Health Institute was the surgeon who changed my life. If you are unable to contact him, find a skilled wide excision surgeon to speak with.

plenty of downtime for the first time in years. I started asking God the questions that I had pushed from my mind for many years—questions ranging from "How does a good God allow us to go through horrible things?" to "Do I really believe feminism is interested in helping me?" I had seen the way the women's movement had intensely focused its messaging on "reproductive rights" (abortion), but they never talked about the disease that I had suffered from. An issue like endometriosis clearly should have been front and center on the feminist agenda, but it wasn't even talked about as a fringe issue. This was the start of my disillusionment.

I had previously embraced almost every demand of modern feminism, with the exception of abortion. The facts of abortion did not line up with the Word of God or my understanding of God and the value of human life. The overemphasis on abortion and the complete lack of attention to women's diseases like endometriosis highlighted a significant difference between my values and the values of the feminist movement. This disparity was the first chink in my armor.

One fateful day as I lay in my room, slowly recovering from my endometriosis surgery, my dad recommended I watch a video called "I'm Pro-Life | Change My Mind" by Steven Crowder.[3] I didn't want to watch it. I didn't want to open my eyes to how big the gulf was between what I believed about abortion and my precious feminist ideals. Maybe I was bored, or maybe I could no longer suppress the curiosity that I had managed to tamp down up to that point. I watched the video and realized that my sorry excuse for "pro-life" views had still been greatly influenced by the feminist movement. I had only thought I was pro-life before, but after just three hours of video from Steven Crowder, every talking point on abortion I had previously

[3]Steven Crowder, "I Am Pro-Life (4th Edition) | Change My Mind," StevenCrowder, March 18, 2019, video, 1:04:51. https://www.youtube.com/watch?v=8nhXQS5UUGQ.

accepted was gracefully dismantled. If I had been so transformed by this video, I could only imagine how much more it would impact someone who was pro-abortion.

I was disturbed. There were other videos in his Change My Mind series that had the potential to undo my entire worldview. The recommended videos in my queue addressed topics like gun control, systemic racism, and Trump. I had been "mostly" pro-life already, so my newfound receptiveness to a genuine pro-life stance wasn't that earth-shattering, but my leftist views on other topics were much more dear to me and I didn't want to think about them deeply and acknowledge their flaws. I liked being an "edgy" Christian. I liked that I shared these views with my beloved feminist community. I liked that people were surprised when they found out I held these views. But against my better judgment, I clicked "play" on the next video.

For years I had been asking God to give me His heart. And while I laid in bed sick, He had answered by awakening my compassion for women, the oppressed, victims of racism, and those facing homelessness. But now I started praying for God to give me a love for truth. And He answered by starting to unravel the many lies that I had mistaken as truth in my pursuit of compassion. One by one, my most tightly held beliefs about the world and politics began to unravel.

I had to cling to the Lord, because everything else in my life was shaking. Steven Crowder's Change My Mind videos were the vehicle God used to lovingly confront my cognitive dissonance. I was deeply offended by some of the videos, but I couldn't deny the truth Crowder presented, so I continued watching. Within a few months, I realized I was no longer a Bernie-supporting leftist. I was a truth seeker, and truth was the thing I wanted most. This timing conveniently coincided with my parents' decision to relocate to the more politically conservative state of Tennessee.

The night after my third attempt at the Miss California USA crown, my parents told me they had decided to move back to the Southeast after six years in southern California. They were headed to Nashville, and I could join them if I wanted. After spending the next few days seeking the Lord about what was next for me, I heard a small voice in my heart say, "Go win Miss Tennessee USA!" So a year post-surgery, I packed up my life and once again moved across the country to a new place.

At this point, I still considered myself a feminist, but I rejected the modern radicalized version. I felt there was a way I could reclaim and rebrand feminism. My challenge now was to get other feminist women to do the same.

JOURNALING:

- Are there any beliefs or values that you hold tightly, to the point of being closed off to God's perspective on those topics? Take a moment to invite the Holy Spirit to reveal any blind spots or areas where you may be resistant to God's guidance. Write down what He reveals to you.

DEEPER DIVE:

- What does it mean to be a pastor? What are your thoughts on women being pastors, elders, or teaching men in the Church? From your perspective, is there ever a time it is or isn't okay? What scriptures inform your perspective? Have any personal experiences influenced your position?

STORIES

Stories have incredible power over the human mind. With story, an author can create new worlds, convey complicated ideas in a way others can understand, and move hearts to feel something that transcends the bounds of the story itself. There have been countless famous stories throughout history—some that built entire civilizations, and others that saw them torn down. Every major religion is built on a story. The story of Moses is the foundation of Judaism and brought the Jewish people back again and again to their homeland after thousands of years of persecution. Likewise, the story of Jesus is the foundation of our Christian faith. His gospel has also formed the bedrock of some of the most successful nations and governments on earth. From England to the United States, the mission of establishing His Kingdom on earth has been spread by His story. Even in our age of technological advancement, few things have as much ability to shape the destiny of political movements, uphold theology, and confuse people on what truth is like story does.

Jesus understood the way stories connect to the human spirit, which is probably why He chose to speak in parables. What mattered more than the parables themselves was the truth conveyed through them. He shared the secrets of the Kingdom through His stories. He opened people's eyes to the immeasurable love of God.

Some stories build, and some tear down. Some worldviews exist to create a new and better world than the one we currently exist in; others exist to criticize and destroy our institutions. For instance, the story feminism tells sweeps in and smashes the institutions of marriage, family, motherhood, femininity, and religion like a wrecking ball. And feminism cannot possibly repair the things it thinks should be torn down.

If you've ever been in a car accident, you know that the insurance company gets to decide if your car is totaled or not. Sometimes they determine it's totaled, not because it can't be fixed, but because they'd rather just give you money toward a new car rather than to pay for the repairs on the old. Feminism has determined that our institutions are a totaled car. Not worth taking the time or effort to repair.

On the other hand, what I am calling women's empowerment seeks to improve the positive aspects of existing institutions by finding the areas that need improvement and working to make them better. This approach allows us to make these institutions better for everyone, including women. Rather than starting from scratch, women's empowerment aims to build upon the good that already exists in areas like marriage and religion. It looks at where we've gone off course as a natural part of the process rather than an intentional plot from God or the patriarchy to destroy women.

Many of the most influential feminist founders had terrible relationships with their mothers and fathers. Many had experiences with sexism in the workplace. Many were victims of sexual assault at the hands of evil men. Undoubtedly these traumatic experiences helped form the harmful storylines about men that are still told to this day. Likewise, if their mothers were toxic, then so was motherhood altogether. If their fathers were deadbeats, fatherhood and the patriarchal family should no longer exist. If a few men chose to enact violence against women, then all men are evil.

Most of us have had terrible experiences with at least a few men. But most of us have also had plenty of equally awful experiences because of other women. Only the feminist story asks us to pretend that the only problematic group of people on earth is men—particularly white men. In reality, it turns out we are all pretty capable of being problematic.

Imagine if we told ourselves toxic stories about every other demographic the way we do with men. We not only tolerate but celebrate the differences that exist in every other people group, but not with men. Instead of men's studies classes and men's history month, we honor the accomplishments and unique way of interacting with the world of every other group.

If we applied feminist theory to racial groups, it would be called racism; to women, it would be called sexism; and to LGBTQIA+ people, it would be called homophobia. Let that sink in. As believers, we cannot allow the other half of God's image-bearers to be subjugated and ridiculed for no other reason than their gender—men or women.

The things we go through in life have a massive impact on our narrative of the world. Just like the early feminists, our personal negative associations with men can form a storyline that prompts us to accept the ideas of radical feminism. If we experience trauma in church, we are more likely to throw out religion all together. If no one in our family has had a happy marriage, we might think the entire institution needs to be ended. We justify allowing our personal experiences to shape our reality by calling it "evidence" when in reality it is only evidence of our own trauma.

Feminism paints a utopian image of a future run by women. Men are quiet and sensitive as they serve our female vision for the future. There are no more wars. Children are raised by the collective, and childbirth is a paid service. But the odds that these untested theories will possibly produce a positive outcome are slim to none.

What if instead, we worked toward restoring what already exists and making that our utopian ideal? We could create a narrative that tells us things can be improved instead of destroyed. Happy marriages where women are loved and cherished by their husbands. Our fertility is celebrated as an integral part of society. Men and women seek to understand the unique ways of thinking that each has. Workplaces support women in their feminine manifestation of fruitfulness. Governments support and incentivize the nuclear family for the stability it brings our nations.

Maybe you don't need feminism but just need a new storyline and a healed perspective of God. Ask yourself if it's possible that your problems with marriage, the patriarchy, men, motherhood, pregnancy, and femininity are because you have not dealt with trauma. Be honest with yourself; there is very little chance that you haven't attributed the difficulties of your own life onto society as a whole. Some of that might even be valid! But it will be impossible to know without attempting to untangle your trauma responses from your embraced worldview.

JOURNALING

What stories are you repeating to yourself about God? About your womanhood? Are they good stories with happy
endings, or tragedies featuring you as the
victim? Reflect on the stories you internalize and write down
any shifts or adjustments you want to make to create more
positive narratives.

_____

_____

_____

_____

_____

_____

_____

_____

_____

_____

_____

_____

_____

Have you ever had a personal experience that influenced your perception of a certain group or even of God? How did it impact your worldview? Just becoming aware of our inner narratives can help us begin to see reality more clearly.

_____

_____

_____

_____

_____

_____

_____

_____

_____

_____

_____

_____

_____

Write down some things about marriage, family, womanhood, etc. that are good. What are some things that could use a change?

_____

_____

_____

_____

_____

_____

_____

_____

_____

_____

_____

_____

_____

_____

_____

Have you ever considered the impact of trauma on your perception of gender roles, marriage, or other aspects of life? Are there things you've been through that might be influencing your views on these topics? How might healing from trauma affect your worldview? Take a few minutes to write down your thoughts.

_____

_____

_____

_____

_____

_____

_____

_____

_____

_____

_____

_____

_____

CHAPTER 2

THE FALSE FLAGS OF FEMINISM

"THE DENIAL-OF-DIFFERENCES VERSION OF WOMEN'S EQUALITY DEMANDS THAT WOMEN WANT WHAT MEN WANT AND BE EVERY BIT AS COMMITTED TO CAREERS AS MEN ARE, BUT BIOLOGY WON'T LET THEM HAVE THEIR WIN."

—KATE O'BEIRNE, Women Who Make the World Worse

In July of 2018, Brett Kavanaugh was nominated for the role of Supreme Court Justice of the United States. As typically happens, there was a lot of backlash from liberals at the choice of Kavanaugh since he was selected by a conservative president. (To be fair, conservatives also tend to have disagreements about justices selected by liberal presidents.) This concern over a more conservative justice being chosen was expected, but what was not were the disturbing stories that began to emerge about Brett Kavanaugh—accusations of sexual assault.

As a deep investigation into the allegations ensued, it quickly became clear that there was no evidence to back up the claims of his accusers. In fact, many of them had obvious political connections to the Democratic Party, which made their stories even more suspect.[1]

Even as Kavanaugh was cleared of his supposed crimes, the American people, with extensive encouragement from the media, had already decided he was guilty. The official outcome of the investigation meant nothing because Brett was a white, privileged, conservative man. In the minds of many, he was guilty with no chance of being proven innocent.

In the 1990s, a similar trial played out against Justice Clarence Thomas. He was famously accused of sexual harassment by Anita Hill. Her accusations, too, never proved his guilt, and he was confirmed to the Court.

These men and their families were put through a gauntlet of character assassination and death threats that could have potentially ended their very hard-earned careers, yet no compassion was extended to them for the suffering they endured. Why? Because our feminist-run culture is quick to vilify men with little concern for whether they are guilty or not.

Early American history is typically framed by the narrative that men kept women oppressed and prevented them from voting until the 1920s. What is often ignored, however, is that men are the ones who voted to give women the right to vote. Furthermore, many women didn't even want the right, as it came along with other obligations like military conscription and bucket brigade for the fire department.[2] Those "evil" misogynistic men of the early twentieth century were the ones responsible for ensuring women were given their constitutional right to participate in the governing process.

[1] Steven Crowder, "BUSTED: 5 NEW Kavanaugh Lies! | Louder with Crowder," StevenCrowder, September 18, 2019, video, 14:08. https://www.youtube.com/watch?v=bdKKwLbeY3A&t=753s.
[2] Lyman Abbott, "Why Women Do Not Wish the Suffrage," The Atlantic, September 1903, https://www.theatlantic.com/magazine/archive/1903/09/why-women-do-not-wish-the-suffrage/306616/.

It is true that evil men have used their power to hurt women since the beginning of time. But that isn't the central narrative of human existence—it's just one storyline. Another equally true storyline is that women have long used their feminine powers to control and manipulate men emotionally, since we typically aren't able to do so through physical strength.

The biblical account of Samson and Delilah is a perfect example. Delilah used her femininity to seduce Samson so he would share the secret source of his strength: his hair. With this knowledge, she sold him out to his enemies and cut his hair so he wouldn't be able to defend himself.

What is clear is that men are not the enemy of women, nor women the enemy of men. Every time that evil men have used their power and strength for evil, you will find that good men have used their power to at least attempt to stop the evil men. What often stands between the vulnerability of a woman and an evil man is the strength of a good man.

During the Nazi occupation of Poland during World War II, Oskar Schindler used his position as a businessman to save the lives of hundreds of Jewish women.[3] The evil Nazi men used their strength to kill and brutally abuse millions of Jews, but still other men stepped in and overpowered or outsmarted them.

In recent history, a young man named Elisjsha Dicken stopped a mass shooting at an Indiana mall when, instead of running away from the sound of gunshots like the rest of the crowd around him, he ran toward it. At only twenty-two years old, he instinctively understood the need to use his firearm skills to save the helpless individuals around him.[4]

---

[3] United States Holocaust Memorial Museum, "Oskar Schindler," *Holocaust Encyclopedia*, last modified February 10, 2023, https://encyclopedia.ushmm.org/content/en/article/oskar-schindler.
[4] Cheney Orr and Brendan O'Brien, "Armed Bystander Credited with Preventing More Deaths in Indiana Shooting," *Reuters*, July 18, 2022, https://www.reuters.com/legal/government/indiana-passer-by-hailed-after-shooting-mall-gunman-2022-07-18/.

Both of these stories are examples that show evil will always exist and manifest itself through men and women, and the strength of good men will always be needed to keep the evil at bay.

JOURNALING:

- Can you think of examples from your own life when men have used their strength and power to protect and support you or other women in the face of evil or injustice?

"Young women at our elite colleges are among the safest, most privileged and most empowered of any group on the planet. Yet, from the moment they get to campus – and now, even earlier – an endless stream of propaganda tells them otherwise. They are offered safe spaces and healing circles to help them cope with the ravages of a phantom patriarchy."

—CHRISTINA HOFF SOMMERS

THE PATRIARCHY

Man has long been seen as the culprit of women's oppression. Feminism told me that men invented the patriarchy in order to oppress me and every other woman on earth. But what if men and the patriarchy are not our enemy, and are actually potential partners in finding fulfillment and protection as women? What if the real enemy is exactly who and what he has always been and uses division between man and woman—the earthly representation of Christ and His Bride—to push us onto the wide path of destruction?

In the story of Sarah and Hagar in Genesis, Sarah doubted God's promise to give her a son, and instead of trusting Him, she listened to the enemy's lies and decided to take matters into her own hands. She offered her servant Hagar to her husband in order to have a child through her. As a wife myself, I cannot imagine the insecurity and certain conflict that would arise from sharing my husband with another woman, let alone allowing her to bear his child. The enemy used doubt and deception to come between Sarah and Abraham in a very real way, and this division brought about a devastating situation. Hagar did give Abraham a son, but the problems this created nearly caused her and her son to both die in the desert and eventually led to the Israeli-Arab conflict of today.

Spirits of darkness, Satan, the enemy—whatever you prefer to call that which is opposed to God and His Spirit—desires to separate the Bride from Christ, and one of his vehicles for doing so is by breaking down the relationships that are meant to reflect God's union with us.

Ephesians 6:12 tells us that our enemy is spiritual forces rather than other people. Our enemy is not men or the patriarchy. Our enemy can manifest in men and in patriarchy and partner with evil spirits, but men and the patriarchy can also partner with the Holy Spirit to bring about life.

With the start of the feminist movement at the turn of the nineteenth century, women began expressing their desire to be seen as equals in society and under the law. Their primary purpose was to gain the right to vote and to have better working conditions. Women at this time faced horrific workplace abuse and had no recognized rights to protect themselves or petition for safety. As this clear mission for justice began to advance and women started to take advantage of opportunities that hadn't been afforded to previous generations, something much less innocent was also beginning.

An idea as subversive as feminism could only have begun in the mind of our adversary. He convinced a bold and promising movement of women that equal value was not enough and that something more radical was required for women to find true "liberation." This is the same tactic that the enemy used to convince little Justice that it was not enough to recognize that the men who took issue with my mom being a pastor had not communicated their position with kindness and grace. I also had to vindicate my mother—and every woman—by proving myself to the entire world as equal to any man. This is a burden that no woman should feel obligated to carry, let alone a little girl.

Women like Betty Friedan, Simone de Beauvoir, Kate Millett, and Gloria Steinem brought to the table ideas that laid the groundwork for the radical feminism of today. These leaders argued that equal protection and provision under US law would never be enough. They claimed something more radical was required. These women argued that we would never be unhindered in our pursuits without the pill; abortion was women's guarantee of freedom; gender was a social construct; and a career was the highest achievement a woman could hope for in life, and everything else should be sacrificed in service of this goal.

Their views were so obviously anti-family, anti-man, and anti-God, yet they slid by. How? They were absorbed into the mainstream primarily through pop culture and the education system.[5] The sexism that many men and women longed to abolish at the first half of the twentieth century predisposed women to be more willing to accept the goals of radical feminism—so long as these goals remained more appealing than the sexism that had prevailed before.

---

[5] James Tooley, *The Miseducation of Women* (Chicago: Ivan R. Dee, 2003).

Much like my childhood reaction to the injustice against my mom when she became a pastor, our culture has followed the same exaggerated trajectory. Instead of identifying and correcting areas of genuine sexism, feminists reacted strongly to any perceived discrimination. For example, if women had not previously been given certain opportunities in science, tech, or engineering, feminists demanded that women be present in those areas, regardless of whether they were qualified or had any desire to be there.

Where does this muddled history leave us as women today? We see many women embracing every extreme claim that modern feminism throws their way, betraying fundamental biological relationships like that of man and woman and mother and child. But we also see a group of women—albeit a minority—who are so disgusted and reviled by the many atrocities of feminism that they have accepted a place of subjugation not only in role but also in value.

In the fundamentalist Christian world, it is taught that women must submit to their husbands, not as a good gift from a loving God, but because they are considered inherently less spiritual and less capable than their husbands. Their belief is that women belong in the home, not because the home is important and worthy of being invested in, but because they, like children, must be obedient and mindless.

These two extremes are a few of the downfalls that bold women of God must try to avoid. We are neither goddesses nor slaves by design.

One of the primary issues with the radicalized feminist movement was that—intentionally or not—it told women that the very things that make them a woman are a hindrance to their "success" and disgusting to culture. If the abortion of our children is celebrated as a sacrament, how can we then look at motherhood with admiration? If men are our great enemy, how can marriage be anything other than a ruse that foolish women surrender themselves to? If we need to change our hormonal and chemical makeup (via contraception) in order to see our dreams come true, how can we regard our bodies as anything other than fundamentally broken? If we must adopt masculine traits to become more aggressive and competitive in the workplace, how will we see our femininity as anything other than a weakness that must be uprooted? If we see masculinity as toxic, how will we ever know how to relate to the masculine heart of God? And if casual sexual encounters mean nothing, how can we value our chastity and view violations in the serious light they deserve?

During my years as a left-leaning feminist, these were the questions that had been slowly creeping into my mind. When I finally began addressing them, I couldn't unsee the issues that existed with so many of the claims of modern radical feminism.

Yehovah—Hebrew for "the God who was, who is, and who will continue to be"[6]—has laid out landmarks for us on the road to becoming women of valor—one of the phrases used to describe the Proverbs 31 woman (see v. 10, TLV). These signposts help us avoid the extremes, but more importantly, they give us a greater understanding of His heart and lead us into a closer relationship with Him.

These landmarks have been co-opted by the enemy throughout history in order to destroy women and the call of God that is upon us. 1 Peter 3:7 calls women "the weaker vessel" of the sexes, and this verse has been used to discredit and belittle the inherent value of women for almost 2,000 years. If we read only this "signpost," we might react by either relinquishing our identity as image bearers or be tempted to think that the Bible is too old and out of touch to have anything of worth to add to our lives today. Our faithful God brings balance and another signal to help us stay on the path of life.

---

[6]Nehemia Gordon, "The Name of God in the Hebrew Gospel of Matthew," Nehemia Gordon, July 4, 2018, 26:52. https://www.youtube.com/watch?v=qgQMeweGjp4.

In 1 Corinthians 1 (as well as several other places in Scripture), God clarifies that He specifically chooses that which is weak to confound the strong—that in our weakness, His strength is more apparent. We might be weaker than our male partners by many metrics (the most obvious being physical strength), but it is our weakness that moves the heart of God to use us as vessels of *His* strength.

This is but one of many examples of the world's understanding of good and bad being out of sync with what God says. God's Word does make clear distinctions between men and women, their roles, as well as their strengths and weaknesses. One might even say that it is impossible to know God fully without knowing, accepting, and loving the masculine and feminine attributes of our humanity. But the Bible never demonizes an entire half of the image-bearers of the Creator! We can read Scripture fearlessly, knowing that His desire and love are for us. It is sometimes uncomfortable confronting the gap that exists between the culture of the world and God's ideals for us, but His path is always good and always brings life!

JOURNALING:

- How do you define "patriarchy"? Do you have a negative or positive association with this word? How does the concept of "the patriarchy" influence your perception of men and their role in society?

- Do you think feminism has taken things too far? What are some things that you do and don't like that feminism has done?

DEEPER DIVE:

- Research the history of marriage and the patriarchy (I recommend searching "History of Marriage by Classically Abby" on YouTube). Find some additional resources and use them to write a brief summary of the importance of patriarchal marriage. Or, if you disagree with those traditional reasons, write your defense here!

THE NARROW PATH OF LIFE

Throughout human history, a trap has existed that seeks to ensnare us. It is disguised as something virtuous and good, telling its victims, "See! You have escaped the evil of the other side!" You may have fallen into this trap too, all the while believing you have safely avoided being like "those people." We've talked a bit about this trap already. We're most vulnerable to it when we are reacting to a negative experience. I fell into the trap of radical feminism in reaction to my mom's ordination being rejected by a few rude men. I thought I was safe because I was far from the sexist belief system that had disgusted me, but I ended up losing balance in the process.

My dad lovingly watched me walk through my personal feminist journey without judgment but also without compromising on the truth. He has always reminded me, "There's a ditch on either side of truth," and this is the trap I've mentioned here. Jesus said, "'Go in through the narrow gate; for the gate that leads to destruction is wide and the road broad, and many travel it; but it is a narrow gate and a hard road that leads to life, and only a few find it.'" (Matthew 7:13–14, CJB)

Jesus was describing Himself as the only path to eternal life with the Father, but he also spoke another significant truth: Do not fall into the trap that exists on either side of the narrow path (the path that leads to life). Truth is a narrow path that is not always easily discernible, especially when you take our human experience and biases into account.

I will use this metaphor of God's narrow path of life and the ditches, or wide ruts, that lead to destruction throughout the chapters of this book. You can imagine yourself walking on a road you've never been on before. You don't know exactly where you are going, but you have your GPS, the Holy Spirit, guiding you. The Spirit helps you pay attention to different landmarks on your journey—landmarks of truth that will help keep you out of the ditches!

If you've ever watched the show *The Office*, you might remember an episode where Michael didn't have a very good GPS and ended up following its commands right into a lake. His GPS was leading him, but he wasn't watching the landmarks. Picking the wrong GPS—the ideology GPS, the political GPS, and others—can quickly land you far from the path God has for your life.

Unfortunately, many who have been hurt by religion would argue that the very idea of a God giving us rules for life is somehow cruel and controlling. We have to remember that the Bible is God's gift to us. He doesn't give us these landmarks because He wants to control us; rather, they are intended to help us avoid steering our new car into the lake.

In his book *12 Rules for Life*, Dr. Jordan Peterson, a clinical psychologist who is also considered by many to be one of the brightest minds of our time, talks about how necessary rules are for the creation of order in our lives and in culture.[7] Far from being tools of tyranny, rules (or, as I am calling them, signposts) have an incredible ability to bring peace, order, and democracy. Tyrannical rulers tend to have "rules for thee but not for me," but it is part of God's good nature to give us both rules and a spiritual guide, the Holy Spirit, to help us navigate His rules in a way that is life-giving.

So how does this idea of following the Holy Spirit on the narrow path apply to our journey as women? Sexism, fear, hatred, anxiety, and disorder are a few of the common things we can find ourselves reacting to. We see on one side of the narrow path the "ditch" of hatred, and in our effort to avoid falling in, we leap right over the narrow path

---

[7]Jordan Peterson, *12 Rules for Life: An Antidote to Chaos* (Toronto: Random House Canada, 2018).

into the opposing ditch. This opposing ditch pretends to be love but is actually just a fear of embracing the messy work of real love, which is helping others walk in truth.

When it comes to sexism, many jump into the opposing ditch of radical feminism—an ideology that has caused huge amounts of destruction to the stability of our culture by attacking the nuclear family. The Holy Spirit brings balance. Not necessarily in a way that always appears balanced, but in a way that brings immense peace. When we walk by the Spirit, we no longer live in perpetual reaction to the horrors around us. Instead, we find a nuanced path forward.

This book exists to help you, as a woman, find the path that leads to life—the narrow, in-between trail that God has hidden for those who love truth. God's design for women is beautiful and perfect. We carry parts of His heart and His image that are lost when we fall into either ditch in the process of figuring out our identity. I pray that you will feel a conviction to challenge your perspectives regardless of your current views—regardless of which ditch you may currently find yourself in. I write as a former feminist who has found so much joy in knowing I no longer have to fight for my voice to be heard or for my value to be known. At the beginning of time, our Father appointed you and me alike as vessels of life, carriers of compassion, and a safe haven for weary souls.

Here are the two ditches that I hope to avoid as we journey together: the ditch of radical feminism and the ditch of fundamentalism. The feminist ditch, as I mentioned before, mostly exists in reaction to the very real limitations and lack of protection that women existed under in the first 200 years of the United States.

Fundamentalism, or the view that God values men more than women, seems to exist both in reaction to the radical feminist movement and as a consequence of chronic misinterpretation of God's Word. Both of these extremes fail to appreciate God's design for us as women and the image of Himself that He placed in us. Together we will discover how God intends for us to manifest His feminine heart in every area of our lives. We will learn to cultivate and grow our femininity regardless of our natural tendencies. And we will experience more of the love of our Father as we reveal His intentionality in creating us.

JOURNALING:

- Write about a time you felt the need to fight for your voice to be heard or your value to be recognized.

- Take a moment to think about the two ditches we talked about: radical feminism and fundamentalism. Which one do you feel more drawn to? Have you fallen into one or the other in the past? How has it affected your understanding of God's design for women?

- Do you need to recalibrate your spiritual GPS? List any other voices that you've allowed to be louder than the voice of the Holy Spirit in your journey as a woman.

SO, WHO'S THE BAD GUY HERE?

There is a common theme in Scripture of distinction. Over and over, we see God contrast the difference between that which comes from Him and is of His Kingdom, and that which comes from the world and is of the kingdom of darkness. This is why I find it extremely unhelpful to identify a person or group of people as the enemy. It is not the people who are the problem, but the spirit they are working under. It isn't men who are the problem, but the demonic spirits that they choose to partner with—spirits of rape, rage, control, self-delusion, etc.

It isn't feminists who are the problem either, but the demonic spirit of feminism. This spirit functions like the spirit of Jezebel that we read about in Scripture. It also has elements of control, self-delusion, rage, hatred, disorder, etc. If you notice, these spirits all function in direct contrast to the fruits of the Spirit of God: love, joy, peace, patience, kindness, goodness, faithfulness, gentleness, and self-control (Galatians 5:22–23). When we see a system operating outside of these ideals, that means it is functioning outside of His Spirit and His Kingdom.

Unfortunately, the very fabric of our society is woven together with feminist propaganda. This makes it very difficult to separate what is true from what we think is true. We are like fish who are unaware that we are swimming in water. In James Tooley's book *The Miseducation of Women*, he reveals just how much of the education system has been shaped by radical feminist legislation.

Much like my childhood perspective that women must prove themselves to the world around them whether they want to or not, a group of dedicated radical feminists worked to enact legislation to ensure that all women would feel the need to prove themselves, starting in grade school. Their expressed goal was to help "close the gap" between men and women in STEM fields (science, tech, engineering, and mathematics), regardless of whether closing that gap would bring fulfillment to women or not. They did not mind if the reason this gap closed was that women were essentially being forced into these fields by the education system rather than because women as a whole had suddenly gained a genuine interest in STEM.[8]

It isn't just the education system that is attempting to shape our natural desires by telling us we ought to desire a career in STEM. Career counselors at schools that receive Title IX funding (the majority of the schools in the US) are not allowed to even mention motherhood as a potential career for the girls that they counsel. This is the consequence of legislation that requires educators to pretend that there is

---

[8]James Tooley, *The Miseducation of Women* (Chicago: Ivan R. Dee, 2003), 31–33.

zero difference in the skills and natural desires of men and women. Slowly, we have seen classes that historically attracted women (home economics and the arts) lose funding as the agenda to "equalize" all things between men and women has been pushed. This has spilled over into every other area of culture.

We are constantly inundated with feminist messaging in books, TV shows, popular music, and a million other sources that reinforces the idea that we, as women, must prove ourselves. We must prove that we are just as capable, if not *more* capable, than our male counterparts. We must be whatever the patriarchy would tell us we are least likely to be.

"The Future Is Female" and "Girlboss" are a few of the slogans we were encouraged to tout when I was competing in pageants. We were literally required to post photos to social media using these hashtags in order to be considered for the crown at a state competition one year. I remember posting photos to my profile and feeling so embarrassed that I had to use these hashtags. It felt like a glaring virtue signal to simply throw around these slogans without connecting them to anything that was *actually* making a difference for women.

To think that this constant messaging has no effect on the choices we make as it relates to our careers and relationships is naive and lacks an understanding of human biology and psychology. We were created by God with a desire to imitate those around us and to desire the things that are considered desirable by our culture.[9] This means that when we surround ourselves with others who are seeking the narrow path of life, we can more easily do the same. However, when we allow culture to be our source of information on womanhood and its many facets, we will inevitably desire what it tells us to desire.

---

[9]"Origin of Mimetic Desire," MimeticTheory.com, accessed June 26, 2023, www.mimetictheory.com/articles/mimetic-desire.com.

Growing up, I had the opportunity to travel all over the world on ministry trips with my parents. I got to experience countless cultures and make friends with other girls my age who lived very different lives than me. When I was on these trips, I loved to go shopping in local stores so that I could wear the fashion that was popular in the country I was in. In Costa Rica, it was sparkly hair clips in bright colors; in the Dominican Republic, I got corn rows with beads; in Korea, it was baby pink nails and tops with lots of bows; and in Dubai, I wore a beautiful black abaya and had henna tattoos done on my hands. I was very quickly and easily influenced by the culture that I experienced around me.

You are likely aware of these obvious ways that culture influences us, but few consider how this idea scales to every part of life. It isn't just the way we dress or do our hair that we adapt from around us—it's the way we perceive men, the things we believe about womanhood, and how we manifest our femininity.

Being influenced by culture in these ways isn't innately wrong. In fact, the way we manifest femininity will almost always have a cultural component. But when we place the value of what culture says about these areas of our lives above what God says, we lose so much of the depth and richness of life that He created for us to experience.

We have to intentionally expose ourselves to His ways of doing things, His definition of womanhood, and His ideas of fruitfulness in order to represent His character as women more than our culture.

I would go so far to say that American culture isn't just influenced by feminism—it has become feminism itself. This means that if you remain neutral in your stance on feminism and remain involved in culture in any real capacity (which means all of us but the Amish), your perspective of yourself as a woman has undoubtedly been shaped and influenced by feminism. This is not necessarily all bad, as they did get

THE FALSE FLAGS OF FEMINISM | 39

some things right, but it will affect your ability to find your identity and definition as a woman in the Lord. It will also undoubtedly negatively affect the way that you view men and the role they play now and have played in history. Neutrality only works when we exist in a neutral environment. Otherwise, like a fish in the ocean, you will inevitably be filled with the water that surrounds you.

If the enemy is spiritual, then what is the goal of our spiritual enemy? I would guess that his goal is for us to be so distracted by the fog of war—feminists vs. the patriarchy—that we don't go to our source, our Father in heaven, for our identity.

JOURNALING

The enemy's goal is to distract us from seeking our identity in God. How have you experienced this distraction in your own life? Write about the importance of turning to God and finding your identity as a woman in Him. What does that mean to you?.

_____

_____

_____

_____

_____

_____

_____

_____

_____

_____

_____

_____

_____

SECTION II
A Woman's First Identity

"And coming to her, the angel said, "Shalom, favored one! YHVH is with you."

—LUKE 1:28 TLV

CHAPTER 3

DAUGHTERS OF GOD

MY DAD

When I was in my sophomore year of college, I started having daily panic attacks. It wasn't clear what triggered these episodes, but they quickly took over every aspect of my life. My friends were clueless as to how to help me, and I was living almost 1,000 miles away from my family. In the days before mental health became something people were open about, I felt lost and isolated in what I was experiencing. Everything in my life was shaking, and I was lost as to how to move forward.

If you've never experienced intrusive thoughts before, they are unwanted and often surprising thoughts that pop into your head, typically about things that are outside of your character. This can make life miserable—especially when the thoughts are connected to your identity as a Christian!

I would wake up and immediately be plagued with thoughts like "What if you accidentally blaspheme the Holy Spirit?" or "What if you drove into the median?" or "What if you committed _____ sin and your family disowns you?" This thought process usually devolved into another string of "what-if" thoughts that scared me. Seemingly against my will, I kept imagining what it would be like if I were some alternate, evil version of myself. I was so distressed by this experience that I even prayed for God to end my life before I could potentially hurt Him or my family.

As sleep deprivation set in, I started questioning how God could possibly allow this level of mental torment with seemingly no cause. Whether directly or indirectly, the enemy used his demonic influence against the natural design of my body to spike my cortisol and dump huge amounts of adrenaline into my system. If you've experienced this before, you know how shocking it is to feel the subsequent depletion of the body and mind.

Enter my dad.

During my first panic attack, I called him on the phone. He was at an airport in Korea but answered his phone anyway. He quickly prayed with me and reassured me that I would be okay. These phone calls became a daily routine for us and often lasted for a few hours. For months, my dad would spend this time on the phone with me, listening to every fear I was processing and never judging me when I would mistakenly blame God for what was happening in my mind. (My mom was a huge part of this season as well, although her support looked different than my dad's).

My dad understood that each of us is constantly in process. Although I was in a momentary mess, my dad trusted that I would eventually land in a healthier place both spiritually and emotionally. As I questioned the very existence of the God with whom I had always had a close relationship, I felt no concern from my dad. He reassured me that I was walking through a necessary season that would eventually end.

I was able to borrow my dad's confidence in God, which helped me avoid getting stuck. I felt no pressure to try and believe exactly as my dad did; instead, I felt his trust in God extend into the trial I was facing. He knew I would be okay, so he didn't concern himself with trying to convince me of what I should or shouldn't believe. My dad didn't try and push his beliefs or convictions on me because he trusted that my heavenly Father would meet me where I was.

I had volunteered to help incoming freshman get an immersive experience at my university (Oral Roberts). My job was to bring a group of about fifty students to a worship night at our campus chapel. As the music began, so did my intrusive thoughts. "How great is our God!" the worship band sang out. Meanwhile, I started spiraling into panic mode: "Do you really believe God is great? What if He isn't even real? What if you are all alone on this planet?" I felt my heart quicken and I lost my breath. I ran out of the chapel, trying not to cry.

But in the entryway, I remembered I had a job to do. I wasn't allowed to leave my students alone inside. I marched back to my seat and recalled something my dad had told me: "You have to get mad at these thoughts that are attacking your mind. It's the enemy!" So I did. I got mad, and under my breath I said, "You are done tormenting me!" Suddenly, after the endless days and weeks of mental torment, my mind went quiet and I felt the peace of God.

I started crying again, this time tears of joy and relief. Then I started laughing while I was crying—my heart feeling light for the first time in too long. My students probably thought I was losing it, but I didn't care. I still had many months of healing ahead of me at that point, but I had reconnected with my heavenly Father, and I knew He was walking with me.[1]

Eventually, I did leave that horrible season of torment behind. I re-encountered the tangible love of God and slowly began to trust Him again. The enemy tried to use that time to traumatize me and damage my perspective of God as my Father, but my earthly father continu-

---

[1] At the time, I didn't understand the intersection of mental health and spiritual attacks. If someone I love was going through something similar, I would recommend a Christian counselor who could address both the spiritual attack and the component of mental health and healing childhood trauma.

ally stepped in and diffused the lies I was bombarded with. I made it through to the other side filled with gratitude instead of trauma. My trust in God's ability to shepherd me through the Valley of the Shadow of Death was strengthened, and my sense of safety in my dad's love also increased. I had suffered, but I was better because of it. This is the difference that good dads make.

My dad's love and affection also helped me avoid dating a lot of the losers I was attracted to, and my closeness to him and my mom helped me avoid the pitfalls of sexual sin that many of my friends had fallen into. I didn't need the attention of random men because my dad, the man I admired most in the world, thought I was brilliant and beautiful.

JOURNALING:

- Let's talk about your dad. What's your relationship with him like? Is he around, or has he been absent? How do you think this relationship has influenced the way you relate to God?

- Now, let's dive into how your relationship with your earthly dad or father figure impacts your dating and relationships. Has it affected the way you approach romantic connections? If you're already married, how has it influenced your marriage? Let's explore how their love, or lack thereof, has shaped your self-worth and the choices you make in the realm of love.

- Share your experiences and insights with a trusted friend or mentor. Open up about how your relationship with your earthly father has influenced your romantic relationships. Be vulnerable and allow their guidance and support to help you navigate these complexities.

OUR EARTHLY FATHER IS NOT OUR HEAVENLY FATHER

If there were a lottery for landing in a family with good parents, I won it. I don't just have a really good father—I have an exceptionally good one. My childhood is filled with memories of him taking me on dates, giving me thoughtful gifts, affirming my worth, encouraging me in my passions, and comforting me in difficult seasons (probably largely thanks to my mom inspiring him). He was and still is extremely present in my life and has become one of my best friends. I can call him for marriage advice, talk to him about my theological questions (even when we disagree), and always count on him to come through when I need practical help. I don't think it's possible for me to overhype what a significant impact he's had on who I am today. I am lucky.

But even with his constant presence and love in my life, there were still ways that he failed me and things about his parenting that I had to work through as an adult. My dad is not God and is, therefore, an imperfect father. I've sometimes projected these insufficiencies in my dad onto how I view my heavenly Father. I often think about how compounded that issue must be for women who did not have a dad like mine.

I have a friend (let's call her Anna) whose dad was an alcoholic and struggled with severe depression most of his life. Anna tried desperately to bring enough joy to her dad's life so that he could be happy again. Her childhood was a constant attempt to "fix" her dad, and she carried the burden of his deep sadness as her own responsibility. When she was in high school, he tried to take his own life—and again two more times when she was in college.

Anna internalized the almost unbearable pain that she wasn't enough to motivate her dad to keep living and overcome his alcoholism. She felt she was somehow responsible for his pain. Her life had been consumed by her pursuit of her dad's approval, hoping that her struggle would somehow bring joy to her father.

When she became a believer, she saw Father God through the same lens that she saw her dad—a man who would require her to constantly perform and be enough in order to receive His attention. Just as she feared being abandoned by her earthly father, she worried God would do the same.

A few years into her walk with the Lord, she could no longer handle the weight of striving for God's love and attention, and she decided to leave the faith. It was only after she sought healing from the emotional damage caused by her father's pain that she began to realize the ways she had projected her dad's issues onto God. As Anna healed and realized she had never been responsible for her dad's happiness and healing, she was able to see that God had always wanted to meet her as a perfect Father—with a love that isn't needy or manipulative. God didn't need her to perform in order for Him to stick around. He wanted to heal her heart and show her what true, unconditional, Fatherly love and protection look like.

If you can relate to the relationship I have with my dad, you are likely in the minority. The number of absent fathers has increased exponentially in the last forty years (see page 59). Maybe you can relate more to Anna's circumstances. If that's the case, I encourage you to move through this section slowly and allow yourself to honestly reflect on what comes to your mind when you think of God as your Father.

JOURNALING:

- What does being a "daughter of God" mean to you? Do you feel like His daughter?

- Let's dig deep here. How did your earthly dad fall short or disappoint you? How have those experiences shaped the way you see God as your heavenly Father?

ENDOMETRIOSIS

After my first few semesters at Oral Roberts University, I transferred to the Fashion Institute of Design and Merchandising because my family had relocated to Southern California. Toward the end of my time there, I had an internship in downtown Los Angeles, just a few blocks from campus.

I also started having more frequent endometriosis flares around this time. One day while I was at my internship, I felt the familiar twisting, fiery pain in my abdomen beginning. I had several blocks to walk back to my car and then an almost two-hour drive home. I was terrified as the pain grew more intense.

I finally made it to my car, pulled into a gas station, and called my dad. Through tears, I told him where I was and that I couldn't drive any farther. I don't remember exactly what happened next because I had to take a pain pill, but I know that my dad drove through Los Angeles rush hour traffic to come rescue me and comforted my heart on the drive back.

Experiencing sudden, intense pain is traumatic, but my dad let me know that he was going to make sure I was okay—that he would always come to my rescue when I needed him. That inevitably spoke to me about Father God. My earthly father's promise to rescue me was the same call I heard from Father God. Just as it says in Joel 2:32 and Romans 10:13, He promises to rescue whoever calls on Him.

Being a daughter of God is a fundamental position in our lives. Before we are our biological or adoptive parents', we are His. Regardless of the circumstances we were conceived in, we did not haphazardly find our way to this planet. We were created with intention and great love. We were created to be His beloved daughters, to be pursued by Him, to surrender to His will for our lives, and to live under the shadow of His protection.

First John 3:1 (CJB) says, "See what love the Father has lavished on us in letting us be called God's children! For that is what we are." Our identity as daughters of God is the first identity we embody as women. For many, the idea of being anyone's daughter is tightly knit to trauma. Others grew up with incredible earthly parents who made sure they always knew they were safe, loved, and cherished. And some had an experience somewhere in the middle.

Regardless of which description rings true for you, we've all been let down by our parents in different capacities. Even their version of perfect love is far from perfect. The gap that exists between the love our parents are able to give us and what perfect love is undeniably shapes who we are as people.

Because our identity as daughters is the first identity we live out as women, it can make or break many other areas of our lives. If our experience as daughters has told us we aren't safe, we will rarely feel safe in our future identities as girlfriends, sisters, wives, and mothers. We don't pick our parents. We don't get to choose if they use their very authority in our lives to build us up into strong women or to tear us down in ways that leave us questioning our identity for the rest of our lives. We don't get to decide if they are healthy or if, instead, our childhood is filled with the reality of their physical suffering.

It is painful to realize that those who were meant to love and cherish you the most instead berated and abused you. If that has been your experience, remember that none of what happened in your childhood was your fault, and neither is the emotional damage you've suffered. You are a precious daughter of the Most High. He loves you perfectly as a father, and His Holy Spirit dwells in us, functioning like a perfect mother. He sees your brokenness and your pain, and He wants to heal every place where your earthly parents let you down. He wants to restore your foundational identity. I genuinely believe this is why God told us to pray to Him as our Father in Heaven—He knew how deeply every heart yearns for the love of a perfect father. He knew that every time we prayed the Lord's Prayer, we would heal that place in our hearts a little bit more:

Our Father in Heaven

May your name be sanctified

May your kingdom be blessed

Your will shall be done in heaven and on earth

Give us our bread continually.

Forgive us the debt of our sins as we forgive the debt of those who sin against us

Do not bring us into the hands of a test and protect us from all evil

Amen.[2]

This prayer helps us reposition our hearts as His daughters, honor His position as King, seek His will to be done above our own, and trust in Him as our provider and protector. As daughters of a good Father, we can relinquish control of our lives and trust the faithful guidance of Him who created us.

When we start to understand our identity as His daughter—a position we didn't have to earn or be worthy of—we gain a unique opportunity to help heal the hearts of His other daughters (and sons) by showing them what family life can be like. If God is our Father, the Body of Christ can really be understood as a family. For some, this looks like literally adopting children as their own, including friends in

[2]Nehemia Gordon and Keith Johnson, *A Prayer to Our Father: Hebrew Origins of the Lord's Prayer* (Bedford, TX: Hilkiah Press, 2005), 175.

family activities, or spiritually mothering those in need of the security and love they missed out on in early life.

JOURNALING:

- Have you ever felt pressure to constantly perform or strive for God's love and attention? What factors do you think are behind this striving mentality?

- Your identity as a daughter of God is a big deal. But are there any wounds or traumas from your earthly dad that make it hard for you to fully embrace this identity?

- It's time to have a heart-to-heart with your heavenly Father. Grab a pen and pour out your fears about trusting Him to father you. Don't hold back—share what your heart truly needs as His daughter.

DEEPER DIVE:

- Using the Lord's Prayer as a template, write a prayer to God as your father. Here is an example:

  Father God in heaven,

  Holy is Your name!

  The name Yehovah that means,

  God who was, who is, and who always will be.

  Be the King of my life, and help me honor Your ways of doing things,

  In my femininity, in my motherhood, in my relationships with men, in my identity as Your daughter.

  Fix my eyes on Your reality, on earth and in heaven.

Provide for my needs as Your daughter today.

Forgive me for all the ways I wander from You

And reject Your knowledge of what is best for me.

Empower me to forgive others who do the same,

Whether they have hurt me or hurt You in the process.

Lead me away from things that tempt me to trust my own judgment over Yours.

Deliver me from every plan of evil set up by the enemy to harm me.

Everything in my life, I surrender to You!
Amen!

"Culture derives from woman - for had she not taught her children to talk, the great spiritual values of the world would not have passed from generation to generation. After nourishing the substance of the body to which she gave birth, she then nourishes the child with the substance of her mind. As guardian of the values of the spirit, as protectress of the morality of the young, she preserves culture, which deals with purposes and ends, while man upholds civilization, which deals only with means."

—ST. EDITH STEIN

ATTACK ON THE FAMILY

One of the most destructive goals of the feminist movement is the mission to dismantle the nuclear family—families composed of a mom and dad and children. This is done by removing the patriarch and head of the family. With no father, there is no nuclear family.

When I have shared these concerns with those in the feminist movement, I have been brushed off as a conspiracy theorist. Maybe you also wonder if I am dramatizing or applying the goals of an extremist minority to the feminist whole.

When I began dismantling my own feminism, I read writings from many of the most famous founders of the modern feminist movement. I couldn't believe what I was reading, and the more I saw, the worse it got. It wasn't a fringe group that wanted to make men obsolete; rather, it was a core value of the feminist movement. Far from the mission of equality that I had pursued as a young woman, these women were fiercely dedicated to ridding the earth of the "poison" of testosterone.[3]

I will let these founding mothers of feminism convince you in their own words that the destruction of men and the family was priority one:

"The complete destruction of traditional marriage and the nuclear family is the 'revolutionary or utopian' goal of feminism."
—KATE MILLETT[4]

"The nuclear family must be destroyed, and people must find better ways of living together."
—LINDA GORDON[5]

---

[3]Germaine Greer, *The Female Eunuch* (New York: Harper Perennial Modern Classics, 2008).
[4]Patrick Fagan and Lauren Noyes, "Why Congress Should Ignore Radical Feminist Opposition to Marriage," The Heritage Foundation, June 16, 2003, https://www.heritage.org/welfare/report/why-congress-should-ignore-radical-feminist-opposition-marriage-0/#pgfId-1033792.
[5] Linda Gordon, "Functions of the Family" in *Voices from Women's Liberation*, Leslie B. Tanner, ed. (New York: New American Library, 1970) 181–88.

"I'm passionately opposed to the nuclear family, with its mom and dad and their 2.4 children. I think it's the most neurotic life-style ever developed."

—GERMAINE GREER[6]

"Marriage has existed for the benefit of men; and has been a legally sanctioned method of control over women . . . We must work to destroy it. The end of the institution of marriage is a necessary condition for the liberation of women. Therefore, it is important for us to encourage women to leave their husbands and not to live individually with men."

—A DECLARATION OF FEMINISM, NOVEMBER 1971.[7]

"I feel that 'man-hating' is an honorable and viable political act, that the oppressed have a right to class-hatred against the class that is oppressing them."

—ROBIN MORGAN[8]

"The proportion of men must be reduced to and maintained at approximately 10% of the human race."

—SALLY MILLER GEARHART[9]

It was horrifying to realize that quotes like these are a dime a dozen. Countless books, articles, and interviews contain these startling ideas because, since the 1960s, this is what feminism has been

---

[6]Germaine Greer, "Germaine Greer Quotes," ThoughtCo, accessed February 7, 2023, https://www.thoughtco.com/germaine-greer-quotes-3530088#:~:text=Selected%20Germaine%20Greer%20Quotations&text=%22Women's%20liberation%2C%20if%20it%20abolishes,let's%20get%20on%20with%20it.%22&text=%22I%20think%20that%20testosterone%20is%20a%20rare%20poison.%22.

[7]Women's Counseling Service, A Declaration of Feminism, (Minneapolis, MN: The Service, 1971).

[8]Robin Morgan, Going Too Far: The Personal Chronicle of a Feminist (New York: Vintage Books, 1978), 178.

[9]Sally Miller Gearhart, Reweaving the Web of Life: Feminism and Nonviolence (Gabriola Island, BC: New Society Publishers, 1982).

about. They abandoned the pursuit of equal protection under the law with bigger plans in mind. We've since put cute catchphrases behind these ideas to hide how violent and destructive they are (e.g., Smash the Patriarchy!).

It is clear to me, from my own life experience, just how important fathers are. As I shared before, my own dad played and continues to play a pivotal role in my life. Even in his imperfect state, the benefits he has brought to my life far outweigh the small amount of difficulty I've faced because of him. I have watched many of my friends without a present father in their lives suffer from deep pain and brokenness. Sometimes this pain manifests as an over-independence and inability to receive help from others, a need for constant sexual attention from men, or like the feminists I quoted earlier, a deep hatred for all men.

If you are a very open-minded person, you might also be open to the idea of dismantling the nuclear family if it had the potential to better society. I applaud your open-mindedness, as I also like to remain open to ideas, regardless of how unusual they might initially sound. However, a quick look at statistics on fatherlessness can quickly shut down any suggestion that a life without mother-and-father-centered families could possibly be beneficial to our world.

Beyond my experiences, studies have confirmed that fatherlessness is linked to poor childhood well-being. According to the National Fatherhood Initiative, not having a father in the home quadruples a child's risk of experiencing poverty, doubles the risk of infant mortality, and increases the risk of teen pregnancy sevenfold—not to mention the increased likelihood of other adverse outcomes such as dropping out of school, experiencing abuse and neglect, and incarceration.[10] What is even more devastating is just how

---

10 National Responsible Fatherhood Clearinghouse, accessed February 7, 2023, https://www.fatherhood.gov/.

many individuals have grown up in homes without fathers. Nearly 60 percent of black children, 31.2 percent of Hispanic children, and 20.7 percent of white children are living absent of their biological fathers according to the US Census Bureau.[11] The number of children living with only their mothers has doubled since 1968, seemingly rising alongside the popularity of radical feminism. However, given the current mental health crisis that the US is facing, fathers are not a luxury but a need.

Any system whose expressed goal is to intentionally create more fatherlessness does not have anyone's best interests at heart—especially not those of women and young girls.

JOURNALING:

- Have you observed the effects of fatherlessness in your life and/or the lives of your friends? How has it influenced your/their attitudes and behaviors?

DEEPER DIVE:

- What are your thoughts on the rise of radical feminism and the decline of the traditional family structure? Do you see any connection there, or do you have a totally different take on it?

GOOD PATRIARCHY

Feminism has long accused religion and the patriarchy of being the source of women's suffering. Borrowing from the post-modern theories

---

[11]Paul Hemez and Chanell Washington, "Percentage and Number of Children Living with Two Parents has Dropped Since 1968," United States Census Bureau, April 12, 2021, https://www.census.gov/library/stories/2021/04/number-of-children-living-only-with-their-mothers-has-doubled-in-past-50-years.html#:~:text=The%20number%20of%20children%20living,Current%20Population%20Survey%20(CPS).

of the twentieth century, feminism uses the idea of a powerful oppressor and a victimized group of oppressed. We've been told that religion and men, especially fathers, have oppressed us and that we must liberate ourselves from them. This has been the explanation for almost every inconvenience we face as women.

A recent trend in Christianity, popular among progressive Christians in particular, is to erase the gendered language that we use to refer to God. Instead of calling God "He" and focusing on His role as Father, there has been an effort to refer to God as "she" or "they"—something I think has and will continue to cause a great deal of damage. This feminist interpretation of Scripture has left the vital role of the father empty in the lives of many.

The logic behind this trend is that God is not gendered in the way we are. In the creation story in Genesis, we are told that both men and women are created in His image. While there is an element of truth to the idea that God's gender is not precisely represented through our earthly biological understanding of gender, it is incorrect to say that referring to Him as "He" and as "our Father" is sexist or harmful. We learn countless things about the nature of God through the Bible, but there is still so much about God that remains a mystery.

While many scriptures use metaphors to compare God to everything from a mother hen to bread, God clearly identifies Himself as Father beyond metaphor. In Matthew 23:9, Jesus says to his disciples, "'[C]all no man your father on earth, for you have one Father, who is in heaven.'" This reality of God our Father is reiterated again and again throughout the Old and New Testaments. But why does it matter so much?

As we read in the previous section, fatherlessness is associated with every kind of societal decline. The need for good fathers is seen and felt deeply in our world today. All the while, feminists have worked hard to erase the one guaranteed good Father that many of us will ever have—

our Father God. By erasing God's gender and His choice to present Himself to us as a father, feminists have only increased the amount of pain and suffering that women now experience.

In the book of Exodus, God first manifested His fatherhood to the masses as He guided His chosen people to the Promised Land. He gave them rules and boundaries, He fed them and protected them, and He helped them work through their many disagreements. His presence as the Father of the Hebrews, and later the Father of Israel, established his people as a bold and strong nation. Imagine if we again started looking to Him to father us in every part of our lives. Imagine the societal transformation that could happen if, even when our earthly fathers failed us, we knew how to look to Him as our loving and perfect heavenly Father.

I have a somewhat bold perspective that I want you to hear me out on. We have been so programmed to view any difference in the roles of men and women as a statement of our worth that we have assumed the existence of the patriarchy is automatically unjust. I hold the unpopular belief that healthy patriarchy benefits everyone and has the ability to create a culture that men and women can both thrive in.

Patriarchy is a hierarchical structure that is organized around male bloodlines. In regular-people speak, this means families are led and protected by strong father figures. A patriarchal family gives all of its members an important role to fill but is spearheaded by the strongest individual—typically the father. He is not the strongest in every way, as in modern times, we understand strength to refer to more than just physical capability. But he is specifically gifted in carrying the burden of financial provision and a sense of stability to the family. Taking a cue from God the Father, a healthy patriarch uses his position to the benefit of the entire family.

If this idea is offensive or difficult for you to reconcile, know that it was for me too! Take a second to breathe. Consider that the concept of healthy patriarchy might actually be a good societal ideal for us to work toward. Granted, not every family will have the ability to make the shift. Some fathers die while their children are still young; some are sick and unable to shoulder the burden of leading the family in a traditional sense; and others are so fundamentally broken that it is inherently better for them to be absent.

When a father fills his ideal role in the family, everyone flourishes. Children feel a sense of security and stability. Wives are cherished and honored. Fathers instill practical skills and life lessons into their children. It is not a tyrannical ruling over others, but leadership modeled after the servant heart of Jesus. This type of family has the potential to remedy all of the pain that initially led to the creation of radical feminism.

JOURNALING:

- Have you ever felt a bit embarrassed or hesitant to identify yourself as a Christian because you don't want to be associated with certain people who also call themselves Christians? How has feminism influenced the way you see other Christians?

- How do you interpret the significance of God being referred to as "Father" in the Bible? How does it shape your understanding of His relationship with humanity?

DEEPER DIVE:

- Imagine a society where healthy patriarchy is embraced and practiced within families. Envision how this could impact individuals, relationships, and communities. Can you picture the positive changes it could bring? Are there any concerns or challenges that come to mind? Take a moment to reflect and write down your thoughts on this vision of a transformed society.

THE WAR AGAINST OUR FATHERS

Clearly a spiritual war is being waged against fatherhood. Like all attacks on the nature of God, it is nothing new, but the current manifestation has primarily come through the radical feminist agenda. This is helpful knowledge as we seek our identity as daughters. We can now see that the deep longing in our hearts for the perfect love of a father will not be satisfied by hating men or removing them from their role as fathers.

The world will always have broken fathers; therefore, we will always need to pursue a greater understanding of our position as daughters of God. But partnering with an ideology whose expressed goal is to further damage the lives of daughters around the world by ridding them of their earthly fathers is not the solution. Even if you disagree with my perspective on good patriarchy, it is clear that attacking the institution of marriage and fatherhood will only cause us more harm.

Instead, let's celebrate every positive display of fatherhood that we see. Let's honor the men who stand between the women that they love and evil men who seek to hurt them. As you date, seek out a man who will be a good father to his future children. If you're already married, focus on encouraging the ways that your husband is functioning well as a father rather than criticizing how he is not. We tend to reproduce the things we are praised for, so praise the ways you do see your husband, father, brother, etc., serving as a faithful father to those in his life.

Sadly, men today are used to being completely villainized by our culture. They are used to being seen as the "bad guy." Taking the time to intentionally build up our fathers/father figures and the men in our lives is very important if we want to counter the damage that radical feminism has done.

JOURNALING

Have you seen any evidence in your life
or in society of a spiritual attack against
fatherhood?

_____

_____

_____

_____

_____

_____

_____

_____

_____

_____

_____

_____

_____

_____

Think about the fathers or father figures who have made a positive impact on your life or in society. Can you recall any specific examples? Let's take some time to honor and appreciate their role. Consider doing something special to show your gratitude, like writing a heartfelt letter, sending a thoughtful text, or even baking something delicious to let them know they are appreciated.

_____

_____

_____

_____

_____

_____

_____

_____

_____

_____

_____

_____

CHAPTER 4

MORE THAN A FEMINIST SLOGAN

"THE SPLENDOR OF THE ROSE AND THE WHITENESS OF THE LILY DO NOT ROB THE LITTLE VIOLET OF ITS SCENT NOR THE DAISY OF ITS SIMPLE CHARM. IF EVERY TINY FLOWER WANTED TO BE A ROSE, SPRING WOULD LOSE ITS LOVELINESS."

—THÉRÈSE DE LISIEUX

A s the second of four girls, for some reason, I always wished there were more of us. Maybe it was my love for the chaos of shared rooms, trying to find music we could all agree on, and even the regular drama we found ourselves working through. The four of us have always been just about as different as can be in both our personalities and values. This has had its challenges, but it is also a beautiful testimony to the power of sisterhood.

Regardless of just how different we are, my sisters and I were, and still are, all very close. There is no need for us to agree on exactly how life should be lived because each of us knows that there is something far more important that bonds us: a mutual desire for the best for each other.

My older sister is a leftist, atheist, feminist TikTok influencer. In case it isn't clear yet, I am the opposite of these things, but somehow, she and I have a close relationship and are able to go to each other for support and advice. We are honest with one another without pushing our worldview onto the other person. We find ways to honor each other and compromise when we spend time together or talk about life in a way that doesn't force our values. This is what healthy sisterhood is meant to be like, but probably something very few of us ever get to experience.

When I started competing in pageants, one of the selling points for me was the sisterhood. I had always imagined that pageant girls were petty and backstabbing—of course, you can find those girls in pageants, just like you can anywhere else—but instead, I found women who were super different than me but who loved and respected me anyway. Our ages and life stages were irrelevant; we all simply connected over our desire to see the best for each other. When a friend would win a title I was hoping for, of course I contended with some personal disappointment, but I also felt excitement that my pageant sister was embarking on a new journey.

When I served as Miss Tennessee USA, I formed a very close bond with Miss Georgia USA and Miss Mississippi USA. The three of us came from different backgrounds, had different values, different interests, and obviously lived in different states, but our connection didn't depend on those things. We quickly developed a sisterhood that transcended the shallow things of life. We truly wanted the best for each other.

When Mississippi won Miss USA, Georgia and I fell to our knees and wept with joy for our friend. It still is one of the happiest memories of my pageant career. Of course, Georgia and I were disappointed we didn't win, but the joy we felt for our pageant sister was so strong that it helped ease our pain. Having sisters taught me the joy of seeing other women succeed. Competing in pageants made it even more real.

When the time came for Georgia to crown her successor, I drove down to Atlanta to support her. We sat in her dressing room and tried not to cry as we processed the end of her pageant career. She took her final walk across the stage while I videoed her like a proud mom with tears streaming down my face. A few weeks later, when it was my turn to pass on my crown, her and Mississippi were there offering me the same emotional support. In fact, in all of our pictures from the day I crowned my successor, our cheeks are tear stained.

Much like other familial relationships, depending on your experiences in life, the concept of sisterhood might sound like a dream or a nightmare. For those who had no sisters, the longing for this closeness with other women is often a deep-felt desire. We see this ache for sisterhood manifest in the popularity of sororities, Girl Scouts, pageants, and even on the playground. But when the bonds of sisterhood are betrayed for competition, the joy quickly turns to trauma. I had my fair share of these experiences once I became an adult as well.

I joined some of my other pageant sisters for a trip to Florida soon after the Miss USA competition. The four of us were some of the few politically conservative women in our Miss USA class, and we had decided to take a trip to the annual Turning Point USA Student Action Summit—a gathering of thousands of conservative students from around the nation. We had an incredible weekend meeting other young people who were passionate about the same things we were. It was a life-giving weekend until we got on social media.

One by one, most of the other women we had competed with, our pageant sisters, had unfollowed the four of us. Their explanation, when asked, was that they refused to see conservative content on social media because these views did not promote a safe place for women of color. As soon as they realized we were not feminist, BLM-supporting leftists, we were not welcome in their sisterhood. It didn't matter that we had formed real friendships with each other, some many years long. I would venture to say it was not even a real sisterhood, as it was conditional upon us all agreeing on our politics.

JOURNALING:

- How would you describe healthy sisterhood in your own words? What do you believe are the essential qualities or elements that make a sisterhood strong and supportive? Share your thoughts on what makes a sisterhood thrive.

- Can you recall a time when you experienced a sense of sisterhood or camaraderie with a group of women who were different from you? Despite your differences, what common ground or shared goals brought you together? How did this experience shape your understanding of sisterhood?

- How do you personally feel when you witness the success of other women, even if it highlights your own shortcomings? How can celebrating others' wins contribute to a stronger sense of sisterhood?

TOXIC WATERS

As a young woman, I somehow managed to avoid much of the drama that can accompany toxic female relationships—probably because my homeschooled friends had been raised not to gossip about other girls. From a young age, I had a distaste for gossip and backstabbing, although I am certain I participated in both. Being homeschooled and a pastor's daughter naturally weeded out many of the relationships that could have really damaged my perspective of sisterhood. Even in pageants, I worked hard to avoid negative conversations about pageant sisters and tried befriending those that others overlooked. I didn't appreciate that the most competitive girls often kept to themselves and refused to talk with the new girls. I tried to treat every woman the way I would treat my older and younger sisters.

Sadly, this is not how most women operate. Many of us have our walls up at the mention of the word "sisterhood" because of the negative experiences we've had with other women. Honest interactions between women can quickly turn into rivalries. Our minds feed us lies of scarcity, telling us there is not enough beauty, wisdom, and nurturing to go around. If we see what we lack in another woman, she becomes a threat to our very identity. Playing off our biological desire to compete for male attention so as to secure the safety of ourselves and our future offspring,[1] the enemy comes and does what He does best—steals our identity through comparison, drowns out the still, small voice of the Holy Spirit, and destroys any chance at attaining the sisterhood we so badly desire.

We often justify our secret (or not-so-secret) feuds with other women by telling ourselves that the anger or resentment we harbor toward them is warranted. It is difficult to interact with a woman who won't bring her authentic self to the conversation or who uses little jabs to boost herself at every turn. Many women have been taught this girlish way of interacting with other women by their own mothers (likely because of their own bad experiences with women). Responding with love in these situations takes not only grace but wisdom too. We must first discover the reason for their competitive energy and then use heaps of self-control to avoid responding in a similar way. Some of the ways the enemy comes against our sisterhood are through gossip, rude sarcasm, cliques, materialism, and an obsession with achieving personal success at all costs.

In Matthew 5:21–22, Jesus tells us that even harboring hatred toward another person is the same heart posture that produces murder. Jesus instead emphasizes the need for sacrificial love toward each other. We are

---

[1]Carrie Gress, *The Anti-Mary Exposed: Rescuing the Culture from Toxic Femininity* (Charlotte, NC: TAN Books, 2019).

told to treat other women as mothers and sisters "in all purity" (1 Timothy 5:2). The word "purity" can often hold certain negative and positive implications for those of us who grew up in the church, so let's explain its place in this verse a little more.

According to Strong's Concordance,[2] the word "purity" comes from the Greek word ἀγνός (or *hagnos*), meaning "exciting reverence, venerable, sacred, clean." In contrast to the many toxic relationships between women we see being promoted by culture, we are told in 1 Timothy to interact blamelessly with one another! Without puffed-up ideas of ourselves, petty annoyances, prideful judgments, or competitive spirits. And definitely without gossiping about one another. In a world that has created an entire culture of pitting women against each other for entertainment (shows like *The Bachelor*, *America's Next Top Model*, and others), it takes a cup overflowing with the fruits of the Spirit to interact in a true spirit of sisterhood, in all purity.

JOURNALING:

- Ready to let go of grudges and embrace a fresh start? Sister, it's time to forgive! Is there a woman in your life, maybe even yourself, who needs your forgiveness? Close your eyes, ask the Holy Spirit to jog your memory, and let's get this forgiveness started!

- Toxic female relationships are difficult! Have you ever encountered situations where sisterhood turned into rivalry or competition? How did these experiences shape your view of sisterhood and female friendships?

- Picture this: a world where every woman supports and uplifts each other, no comparisons, no competition. Can you recall times when you've compared yourself to others or felt a twinge of jealousy? What

[2]David Guzik, "Study Guide for Hagnos," Blue Letter Bible, accessed February 7, 2023, https://www.blueletterbible.org/.

are some ways you can break free from that mindset of scarcity and cheer for your sisters instead?

DEEPER DIVE

- Explore the role of self-control and grace in responding to negative interactions with other women. How do you typically respond to situations where another woman is not bringing her authentic self or engages in competitive behaviors? How can you cultivate wisdom and grace to navigate these situations?

- What do you think it means to interact blamelessly, in all purity? How can you let go of pride, judgments, and a competitive spirit in your relationships with other women? How can you actively promote a culture of sisterhood in your own life? Write a prayer asking the Lord to give you a strategy to overcome areas where you need more of His grace.

"Where there is goddess worship, radical feminism isn't far behind, and vice versa."

—CARRIE GRESS, The Anti-Mary Exposed

GODDESS CULTURE

On the other side of the ditch of girlish immaturity and competition lies the ditch of what I will call "goddess culture." In response to the poisoned waters of sisterhood, a spiritual movement has arisen that leaves the Holy Spirit out of things altogether. Ranging from practices as innocent as "self-care" to the more out-there "goddess circle," the desire to understand our own feminine mystery chases many of us down. When we don't have a deep understanding of God as the source of the answers to who and what we were created to be, we come up with our own, often strange, answers.

Typically, this search results in the worship of the "divine feminine" or "inner goddess" that is said to dwell in us all. Unfortunately, by not providing engaging dialogue on issues like true femininity and allowing for deep questions, the church has allowed a vacuum to form that has led to the idolatry of our womanhood. In some cases, this movement can romanticize the sisterhood dynamic to such an extent that it becomes sexual. The famous Greek poet Sappho lived on the island of Lesbos, where she sexually abused young women and girls in order to "teach them" the "special" bond that they could have by sexualizing their interactions with one another.[3] We see very similar tactics being used today to confuse young women about their identity, purpose, and the perfect feminine design God has placed in us.

I am not here to demonize anyone who has same-sex attractions, but I think it is vital that we understand some of the cultural and spiritual conditioning that might be contributing to confusion around our sexual identity. We've been conditioned by feminism to question our sexual and gender identities, but not to question what might have contributed to the confusion in the first place.

As we've discussed before, we imitate what we see normalized around us. This is especially true of girls and women, as we are psychologically more susceptible to something called "social contagion." Social contagion is seen clearly in the way everything from fashion trends to TikTok dances spread. It is also seen in the recent 5,337 percent increase in young women seeking gender reassignment surgery

---

[3] Jim Powell, trans., *The Poetry of Sappho* (Oxford: Oxford University Press, 2007).

in the UK—a trend that clearly exceeds what would be expected from purely organic growth.[4]

The early feminists were passionate advocates of "goddess culture" and the sexual confusion that often comes with it. Kate Millet, one of the most notable feminist leaders of the twentieth century, was known to host parties with other feminist leaders where various rituals involving human blood and orgies were commonplace.[5] Unsurprisingly, this demonic behavior blurred all lines of decency for Millet, who eventually tried to coerce her own sister to have sex with her. Much like Sappho, Millet's ideas of "sisterhood" always involved perversion. It is no wonder that generationally, as radical feminism has been embraced by more women, so too has the percentage of women who consider themselves to be a part of the LGBTQIA+ community.

The journey from girlhood to womanhood is one that few women would choose to relive. Changing bodies, raging hormones, and competitions for male attention are all par for the course. I felt weirded out by the physical changes I was going through during puberty and even more horrified by the start of my period. Puberty is a confusing time for almost everyone, as evidenced by my awkward old Facebook photos, but now we have created an avenue for even more confusion. Instead of telling young women that it is normal to feel confused and emotional during these tumultuous years, we tell them that perhaps something is deeply flawed within them.

Young girls today don't get the benefit of simply riding out the awkward years in commiseration with their friends. Feminist ideology has introduced new options into the hormonal swirl. "Perhaps the

---

[4]Sally Lockwood, "'Hundreds' of Young Trans People Seeking Help to Return to Original Sex," *Sky News*, October 5, 2019, https://news.sky.com/story/hundreds-of-young-trans-people-seeking-help-to-return-to-original-sex-11827740.
[5]Carrie Gress, *The Anti-Mary Exposed: Rescuing the Culture from Toxic Femininity* (Charlotte, NC: TAN Books, 2019).

confusion you're feeling means you are trans, non-binary, a lesbian, or all of the above! And if anyone in your life questions your new-found identity that has been largely influenced by the recent dump of hormones into your bloodstream, they are toxic and misogynistic."

For many early feminists, lesbianism wasn't just a solution to the human need for companionship; it was meant to replace sisterhood as a whole. They didn't just feel that lesbian women needed a seat at the table—they also saw a future in which all female relationships were sexual. Somehow, the idea that women could have close bonds of friendship without mixing in sexuality was not a possibility in their minds. Alison Bechdel wrote, "Feminism is the theory. Lesbian-ism is the practice."

Remembering that this agenda is baked into the feminist bread helps us realize how important our position on feminism is in form-ing our female friendships. The enemy would love to either pull us into toxic gossip and competition with other women or bring sexual confusion to the essential bonds of sisterhood. Being a good friend to the women in your life in a culture that glorifies two toxic extremes requires intentionality and the guidance of the Holy Spirit.

JOURNALING:

- Have you noticed a lack of the church talking about true feminini-ty? Instead, we've seen alternative spiritual movements take center stage. How has this led to idolizing women? Have you ever sought answers about your femininity in unhealthy or extreme ways?

- As you entered womanhood, did you feel overwhelmed by the shift from girlhood? Did you ever feel that something was deeply flawed within you due to the challenges that came with puberty? What do you wish you could go back and tell yourself?

- Let's talk about being intentional and guided by the Holy Spirit in your friendships with women. How can you cultivate healthy, supportive bonds in a world that promotes toxic dynamics? Invite the Holy Spirit to navigate the complexities of female relationships with you right now!

BEING A GOOD FRIEND

I will not pretend to be an expert on friendship, as I have had many failures on this front in my almost three decades of life. I have betrayed and been betrayed by those I love. I have allowed competitive energy to define relationships. I have been bullied and bullied others. And my less-serious friendship offense is how slow I am at responding to my texts, as evidenced by the sixty unread texts in my inbox.

My older sister had a friend that would come over to help her babysit us younger kids. Maybe it was because she was the youngest in her family, or because she was trying to show off for my sister, or because she just really didn't like me, but every time she came over, she would say things that tore me down inside. She would tell me how annoying I was and how miserable I made her. I was crushed that my older sister and her friend would see my entirety as "annoying," and in response, I started acting out toward our neighbor.

She was younger and very quiet, so she was an easy "target" for my insecurity. I didn't mean to bully her, but something about how small I felt because of the way my sister and her friend treated me made me want to treat someone else the same way. The height of my mean treatment of our sweet little neighbor was me tying her shoes together. Understandably, her parents were very angry, and I was embarrassed.

Despite this incident, my childhood best friend has faithfully stood by my side for almost thirty years. When I got married, she drove five hours from Atlanta to come help my new husband and I with some home renovations. She made the trip again when I found out I was pregnant and helped me paint the nursery and build the crib. She's not just there for me in practical ways, though. She also always encourages me in my walk with God, refuses to gossip, and keeps me laughing with her stories.

The reality is that most of us have been the brunt of someone's joke and responded by making them (or someone else) the brunt of our joke. But we have also likely experienced at least one friend who continually goes the extra mile for us. Here are some lessons I have learned along the way that have helped me become less toxic and enjoy my female friendships more.

- Refuse to gossip.

- When you are feeling competitive with a friend, do some soul-searching. Is the competitive energy because you are feeling insecure? Or perhaps your friend is projecting it because she is. Address it!

- Have a policy of honesty with your friends. We often sugarcoat and even bend the truth in order to make our friends feel good. You don't need to be a jerk, but don't lie to them when the truth can bring them a breakthrough and peace.

- Befriend those who others won't.

- Don't have close friendships with truly toxic women. These are relationships where you have done all of the above but have not been met with authenticity in return. Whatever benefit you think you're getting from toxic relationships, it's not worth it!

- Don't require people to be just like you in order to be their friend.

- Don't call friends toxic simply because they tell you the truth. If they have a history of being a faithful and trustworthy friend, it is worth listening to the painful truths they will sometimes share with you.

- Don't allow goddess culture to bring sexual confusion into your female relationships.

If you are struggling with same-sex attraction, you are not alone! There are many other women who love the Lord who have gone through or are going through the same thing. Unfortunately, there tends to be a lot of shame attached to this particular struggle. Our culture has conflated our sexual attraction with our very identity.

In the world today, to be same-sex attracted means your identity is a gay person. This is as ridiculous as saying that your identity is defined by any other natural appetite that you have. You love chocolate, so you are a chocolaterian (I just made that word up!); you watch too much TV, so you are a TV addict, etc. Defining ourselves by our appetites, sexual or otherwise, means we are embracing an identity based on something other than being a child of God.

Just because you struggle does not mean you are defined by something. We all struggle with sin of various kinds, but by the power of the blood of Jesus, we have been set free from a life of enslavement to that identity. We now get to put on His righteousness as our own, and His Holy Spirit empowers us to overcome the sin that seeks to entrap us.

For some people, choosing celibacy has been the solution to overcoming their same-sex attraction. For others, a period of emotional healing helped them enter heterosexual marriages that were fulfilling and redemptive. No matter what your path forward looks like, your sacrifice of this identity to the Lord is nothing but beautiful to Him. You are not rejected or a source of shame for the body of Christ. You are a light and testament to the transformative power of His love.

Here are some resources I recommend if you are struggling with same-sex attraction:

- Read Jackie Hill Perry's book *Gay Girl, Good God*.

- Find someone you can be accountable to who doesn't struggle with the same sin. Have them help you come up with practical boundaries that create patterns of freedom in your life. Maybe you need to take a break from social media, avoid sleepovers with certain female friends, or you need a coping mechanism for when you're feeling tempted to watch porn, etc.

- Get counseling or psychotherapy that helps you determine if your same-sex attraction is coming from broken places in your heart and mind, or if maybe you are simply naturally more masculine.

- Cultivate your femininity, even if it feels unnatural.

JOURNALING:

- Think about that childhood bestie who's been your ride or die. How has their support and loyalty shaped your life? How have they practically helped you, encouraged your faith, and brought you joy and emotional support? Time to send them a heartfelt message to thank them for always being there!

- Reflect on the concept of femininity and its cultivation. How do you define femininity? Have you ever felt disconnected from your femininity? How can you embrace and nurture your femininity, even if it feels unfamiliar or challenging? What are the potential benefits of cultivating femininity in your life?

DEEPER DIVE

- Get your sticky notes ready! Make a list of actionable steps you can take this week to cultivate and celebrate your God-given femininity. Write each step on a sticky note and put them on your mirror. Maybe that looks like letting your boyfriend pay for your date, dressing more femininely, or asking the Holy Spirit to help you honor your feminine traits.

WHAT YOUR FRIENDS AREN'T TELLING YOU

If there's one thing I have learned in the last few years, it's how little Millennial and Gen-Z women know and understand about men. And until recently, myself most of all. Our ignorance destroys our relationships, self-esteem, and attempts at dating, and it feminizes a generation of men.

Spending my childhood surrounded by women gave me a decidedly feminine lens that I saw the world through. My understanding of "normal" was distorted, which made life a lot harder than it needed to be. I found myself sabotaging my relationship with my boyfriend (now husband) in ways that I didn't initially recognize as sabotage, and when he called me out on my behavior, I thought he was the crazy one. Oops!

If no one has told you this already, men and women are SO different. Our biology affects every facet of our lives, from the ways we think and communicate to everything in between. When we interact with men the same way we interact with women, we will frustrate our brothers, friends, fathers, and partners and ultimately frustrate ourselves.

I say this not to be contentious but because I desperately want to see you, my sisters, thriving. Radical feminism has taught us to be hypercritical of our male counterparts. It has deprived us of the tools we need to better relate to men and has instead encouraged us to tear men down. This has prompted a self-righteous attitude when interacting with the parts of men that are different from us as women. It has also distorted our view of reality, causing us unnecessary hurt in our relationships.

Maybe some of the very things we've been told to hate in men are the things we will love and appreciate the most in them if we change our perspective. It's time for us to drop our self-righteous attitudes toward the men in our lives and humbly examine areas where we can grow instead.

One of the biggest issues with this distorted view of men is it causes us to focus on the wrong things in the dating process. Instead of focusing on the character and integrity of our partner, we get lost in the weeds of HOW they say things and if they are emoting the way we would prefer. Living with a woman will naturally help a man grow in his ability to be sensitive and communicate in ways that we prefer, but what rarely changes is a man's character. Does he work hard, is he honest, does he honor you, does he honor God (regardless of whether his relationship with God looks like yours)? Those are the things that truly matter.

None of this advice applies in a situation involving abuse. Abuse is never okay or excusable. If the man in your life is not abusive and simply deals with the issues that we all face as humans, try focusing on your own faults and how you can grow rather than harping on his. Our men want to be worthy of our love, and your self-growth, along with a new humble attitude in your interactions, will call out the inner king in the men around you.

JOURNALING:

- Have you ever felt like you're in the dark when it comes to understanding men? How has it affected your dating game, relationships, and even your self-esteem? Maybe, like me, you never considered that men and women think and behave differently at a biological level. Take time to ask the men in your life about their experiences trying to relate to women. You might just gain some eye-opening insights to write down!

- Okay, let's get real. Have you caught yourself being hypercritical of men or tearing them down? It happens, but it's time for a change. What are some ways you can embrace a more humble and open-minded perspective?

YOU CAN ONLY CHANGE YOU

If you're in a relationship with a good, godly man but find yourself struggling, the best thing you can do is work on yourself. It is our natural instinct to notice what could change and improve in our partner, but by focusing on his weaknesses, we risk shutting down our influence in his life.

> Better to live on a corner of the roof
> than to share the house with a nagging wife.
> Proverbs 21:9 (CSB)

None of us want to be constantly reminded of our areas of weakness. There is almost nothing more demoralizing. However, nothing motivates a man to get himself together like the desire to be worthy of his woman's love. By taking an honest look at your strengths and weaknesses and working to develop what needs to be developed, you will inevitably inspire your partner to rise up and do the same.

Share with him what you're working on and ask him to help hold you accountable. It might suck at first to have him point out when you're being impatient or when he's feeling controlled by you, but two beautiful things will happen: You will find yourself humbled and realize you really should confront your own weakness before pointing out his, and your man will also feel honored that you care enough to let him tell you hard truths.

Men's relationships with God often look very different than ours do. It's all too easy to look at the way our partner interacts with God and assume that He is less close to God than we are. I used to genuinely think that a man not raising his hands in worship at church meant he wasn't as good of a Christian. I cringe just saying that.

Just as men and women have different ways of interacting with every other facet of life, how we approach a personal relationship with God is no different. The only real way to know if your man is solid with God is to look for evidence of spiritual fruit in his life. Luke 6:43–45 emphasizes the point that a good tree will bear good fruit. Plenty of men talk a good talk about God, but behind closed doors, they choose sexual immorality, abuse, manipulation, and pride.

When I was in ministry school, I met countless men who were having supernatural experiences with God, who would weep with arms stretched wide in worship, and who were chosen to be leaders in our class. They went on to completely abandon their relationship with God, and some later admitted their outward religious zeal had been an act that they got swept up into in the heat of the moment.

I recently ran into a friend who had been in a small group with me in ministry school. We were at an event for conservative Christians, and both of us expressed our shock at seeing the other there. "I can't believe there's someone from our group who is still walking with God, let alone conservative!" he expressed to me. We both recounted how many of our dearest friends from that season of our lives had decided to deconstruct their faith and values until there was nothing left.

While many godly men will have very public ways of expressing their love for God, that is not a requirement. My husband, for instance, is very reserved in every area of self-expression, including expressions of faith. But it's still very apparent that his relationship with God is unshakable, produces good fruit in his life, and informs the way he leads our little family.

Don't require your boyfriend, fiancé, or husband to express his relationship with God like you do. Instead, find ways to affirm his unique way of connecting with God and appreciate the ways he prioritizes God.

Not all men, but many of them, have been characterized by women as insensitive, emotionally unintelligent, blunt, overly aggressive, rude, lacking self-awareness, forgetful about important details, etc. It's so important to realize that every trait has a positive manifestation and a negative one. When we focus on the negative ways these traits manifest in men, we lose sight of some of the amazing and unique strengths they possess that we don't.

Instead of regarding men as insensitive and emotionally unintelligent, consider that they may simply be more pragmatic, which can actually help bring balance to our intuitive and emotional perspectives. Instead of judging your man as overly aggressive toward other men, acknowledge his efforts to protect and defend your honor as an expression of love. You can put a positive spin on almost every seemingly negative trait that men embody. It's up to us as women to intentionally highlight the good men in our lives—to value them, honor them, and help empower them to be the fathers and world changers they were created to be.

For example, my husband is not great at communicating his emotions verbally, but he is constantly doing little things to demonstrate his love for me. When I stopped demanding that he express his love in the way that I wanted, I learned to recognize and appreciate the efforts he had been making all along to express his love in his own way. He is growing in his ability to speak my love language, but in the meantime, I can only change me. When I am steadily noticing and thanking him for how he is loving me, his heart softens toward me and he becomes even more loving! But I've also noticed that I feel more loved when I am doing this because I am intentionally showing gratitude for love that I wasn't previously noticing.

JOURNALING

Do you tend to focus on your partner's faults and areas for improvement? How has this impacted your relationship and your influence in his life? Are you a voice of criticism or a voice of encouragement to him?

_____

_____

_____

_____

_____

_____

_____

_____

_____

_____

_____

_____

_____

_____

Are there ways you could humble yourself in your relationship with your partner, father, or brother? Make a list of a few things you want to work on and share them with the men in your life. Ask them to hold you accountable.

_____

_____

_____

_____

_____

_____

_____

_____

_____

_____

_____

_____

_____

_____

Consider your perception of your partner's (or father, brother, grandfather if you aren't married) relationship with God. Have you ever judged or compared his way of connecting with God to your own? Remember, it's not about his external expressions of faith, but the spiritual fruit his life yields. So, take a step back, sister, and consider how you can affirm and appreciate his unique relationship with God.

_____

_____

_____

_____

_____

_____

_____

_____

_____

_____

_____

_____

_____

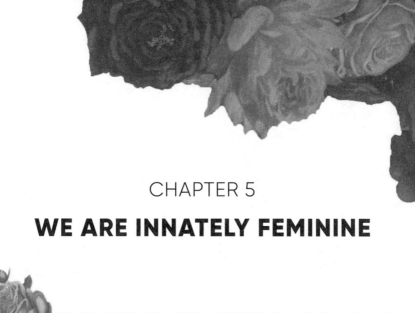

CHAPTER 5

WE ARE INNATELY FEMININE

"INSTEAD OF ASKING, 'WHAT SHOULD A WOMAN DO—WHAT IS HER ROLE?' IT WOULD BE FAR MORE HELPFUL TO ASK, 'WHAT IS A WOMAN—WHAT IS HER DESIGN?'"

—JOHN ELDREDGE, *Captivating: Unveiling the Mystery of a Woman's Soul*

Accepting our place as victims is an important part of the feminist mission. After all, if we aren't victims of the oppression of men, the patriarchy, and motherhood, then we have actual power to improve our lives and, therefore, don't *need* feminism. I view the feminist movement as a sort of bully, convincing us that we have no power and no ability to make our lives better.

God's design for us is far from the victim status that we have often relegated ourselves to. He has empowered us with His image and His Spirit.

"Women's empowerment" is what the feminist movement claims to be interested in. Ironically, it is more interested in securing our status as permanent victims than in achieving true empowerment. They tell us that aborting our children, acting like men, and sleeping around are all empowering—just go to the annual Women's March and this becomes clear.

The definition of "empowerment" is the process of becoming stronger and more confident, especially in controlling one's life and claiming one's rights.[1] Abortion rights don't empower us as women; they empower us to end our pregnancies. Encouraging sexual "freedom" while failing to talk about the psychological and physical significance of sex doesn't empower us as women; it empowers us to open our lives to the messiness that sexually bonding with multiple partners can bring.

God actually empowers us to be powerful women. He gives us important roles in our world and in His Kingdom. He gives us a piece of His image to carry. He gives us the ability to make our corner of the world more beautiful. He gives us fruitfulness and a mandate for motherhood (Genesis 1:28)—both spiritual and biological.

The victimhood mentality that feminism embeds in the minds of its adherents doesn't limit itself to our womanhood. My generation and the next often describe their life circumstances as a series of events that they are powerless over. "Why is this happening to me?" is the attitude of many. It is true that past abuse is a horrible violation of our bodies, minds, and spirits that we are not responsible for! But there is a difference between experiencing abuse and experiencing the normal struggles of life. Normal struggles are not an excuse for us to wallow in self-pity and refuse to grow.

Consider what the Bible has to say regarding life's difficulties and challenges:

> "But he said to me, 'My grace is sufficient for you, for my power is made perfect in weakness.' Therefore I will boast

---

[1] Merriam-Webster.com Dictionary, s.v. "empowerment," accessed February 7, 2023, https://www.merriam-webster.com/dictionary/empowerment.

all the more gladly of my weaknesses, so that the power of Christ may rest upon me. For the sake of Christ, then, I am content with weaknesses, insults, hardships, persecutions, and calamities. For when I am weak, then I am strong."

—2 CORINTHIANS 12:9–10

"Not only that, but we rejoice in our sufferings, knowing that suffering produces endurance, and endurance produces character, and character produces hope, and hope does not put us to shame, because God's love has been poured into our hearts through the Holy Spirit who has been given to us."

—ROMANS 5:3–5

"Little children, you are from God and have overcome them, for he who is in you is greater than he who is in the world."

—1 JOHN 4:4

"Count it all joy, my brothers, when you meet trials of various kinds . . ."

—JAMES 1:2

How different is this biblical perspective on facing hardships in life compared to what our culture has popularized? Like all things, there is a balance to be found. We want to have compassion on ourselves when we are doing hard things. But we also don't want to allow our very identity to be affected by our trials.

We face trials because we are humans existing in a broken world, not because life is out to get us. All of life is constantly in atrophy—things are in a continual state of wasting away. Your uneaten food will rot, your clothes will get stains and holes, your car will break down, your roof will need to be replaced, your relationships will encounter conflict. Contrary to what we've been told, this is normal.

One of the keys I've discovered to becoming happier and feeling more empowered as a woman is to accept this more realistic view of the world. Optimism is made more resilient by accepting and expecting things in life to go un-ideally! Don't act surprised or take this personally. We have to acknowledge that what is not maintained will decay.

When I was little, I had a pet goldfish that lived in a little bowl that I hated cleaning. Unfortunately for little Nemo, my dislike for cleaning his glass home probably played a role in his early death. Just like a goldfish bowl, the things and relationships in our lives will deteriorate without regular maintenance.

All too often I hear others choose to embrace a perspective of reality that feeds depression, anxiety, and hopelessness. Our culture has convinced us that getting a flat tire is bad luck, facing a health challenge is God's punishment, and encountering a cat-caller confirms that all men are disgusting. We have allowed ourselves to become victims of the mundane because our expectation of "normal" is so far from reality.

We are not victims of our womanhood. We face real and unique challenges as women, but so do men.

We've accepted a false gospel as believers that tells us, "If God loves you and you have enough faith, your life will be easy." Subliminal messaging tells believers they are outside of the will of God because they aren't rich, aren't healed, or aren't otherwise thriving. This is counter to the central message of contentment found in both testaments of the Bible. Scripture repeatedly tells us to EXPECT not only the normal trials of life but also persecution and difficulty. The beauty is that we have a loving Father, Savior, and comforting Spirit walking through these experiences with us. He is constantly working to bring redemption and purpose into the ordinary and extraordinary trials of life. The sign of

His favor and love is not that our lives are going "smoothly;" rather, it is finding joy IN the mundane and the trials.

His empowerment is especially evident in our trials. He helps us face heart-wrenching realities with grace because His empowerment isn't just a tagline. He empowers us through the physical but also the spiritual—giving us everything we need to accomplish what He has asked of us in our given circumstances.

JOURNALING:

- Describe what an empowered woman looks like to you. How does she dress, speak, and think?

- Do you feel like you are an empowered woman? Why or why not?

- How is God empowering you today?

DEEPER DIVE

- In what ways have you felt like a victim as a woman? What does God say about these areas in which you've felt marginalized? What does He want to speak to your heart?

- In what ways has God empowered you according to His design? Reflect on the roles and responsibilities He has entrusted to you as a woman, both in the world and in His Kingdom. How does embracing this empowerment differ from the narrative often associated with feminism? How can you rock your God-given power and purpose in a way that's uniquely you?

- Write a psalm to the Lord. Begin by sharing ways you've felt disempowered and broken as a woman, ask for His perspective, and finish with praise for His perfect design in creating you!

GOOD MOTHERS

"The woman's soul is fashioned as a shelter in which other souls may unfold."

—ST. EDITH STEIN

It's hard to put into words just how much influence a good mother can have on our lives. My own mom's presence in my life feels so integral to my reality that it often goes unnoticed. They say that children don't even realize that their mom is a separate person from them until they are two years old. I tend to think that many of us never fully grasp that reality.

A good mom allows us to orient our entire reality around her; to be fed by her physically throughout infancy, and then emotionally and spiritually for the rest of our lives. And to be a truly good mom, she has to offer herself completely to her children while working to make herself obsolete—helping her children leave the nest and equipping them with the life skills necessary to do so.

I can't think of another role in life that requires both a complete willingness to sacrifice yourself for other people while relinquishing all power over who they become.

My mom has existed as a living sacrifice for my siblings and me. She continually makes herself available to us while holding each of us very loosely. Her love has been as unconditional as a human's love can be.

I started competing in pageants around the same time that my endometriosis really started affecting my life. I was a college student, involved in school clubs, developing my pageant platform, fundraising for my pageants, and trying to cultivate an online following. All of this was rudely interrupted by the almost constant pain I was living in.

My mom would faithfully care for me each month on my period as I laid in bed, unable to do anything for myself. She helped me manage my time so that I wouldn't get behind in school and encouraged me to keep pursuing my pageant goals in spite of my sickness—both things that were impossible without her help.

One day I sat at our dining table, surrounded by school projects, and had a breakdown. I was so overwhelmed by trying to finish my homework, purchase my wardrobe for an upcoming pageant, and stay involved in extracurriculars while I was suffering physically. My mom sat with me, helped me schedule out all of my school work, proofread my honors society president application, and planned a time to take me shopping for a pageant gown—all on top of her own pressing schedule. Instead of leaving me to figure it out by myself, or even discouraging me in the many things I was pursuing, she encouraged me that I could do the hard things that were in front of me.

I ended up doing so well with my new time management system that I had an almost perfect GPA, I won the local pageant I had been preparing for, and I became president of the honors society. But the day after the pageant, I physically crashed. I was in excruciating abdominal pain, and yet again, my mom rescued me by helping me contact professors, bringing me food in bed, and being a constant source of encouragement.

She spent months researching possible treatments for my endometriosis and paid for them so that I could focus on fundraising for my pageant journey. After a few months of searching and praying, the Holy Spirit led her to a webpage about a rare and special surgery for endometriosis. The procedure, called wide excision, has an exponentially higher success rate than the typical ablation done on endo. But the recovery is longer.

My mom drove me from Los Angeles to San Jose to have the life-changing surgery. The eight-month recovery that followed was brutal but my mom was my strength every step of the way.

Those were some of the darkest days of my life, but my mom didn't let the darkness keep her from being there for me. Not only did she care for me in every tangible way in those months—feeding me, helping me go to the bathroom, keeping track of my medications all day and through the night—but she also cared for my heart in a way that helped heal my trauma.

My mom listened as I processed my pain and fear, and she helped guide and direct my thoughts. She sat with me when I cried, she prayed for me when I was lost, and she never stopped reminding me of how strong I was. Words can't possibly describe how much I needed her at that time, and how grateful I am that she never failed to show up.

This is the work of a godly mother. She faithfully nurses the hearts of her children back to health as she nurses their bodies. She forgoes her own needs for sleep and stability in order to ensure these things for her children.

As I write about my mom, I have tears streaming down my face. I am still deeply impacted by my mom's ever-present love five years later.

When I began feeling God calling me to write a book, my mom was immediately supportive. Not just in words, but in action. When I was concerned I wouldn't finish writing before the arrival of my baby in just a few short months, she planned a trip for the two of us.

I am currently sitting in my grandparents' beach condo, being waited on by my mom, who has plenty of other more important things that need her attention. But instead of giving her time and attention to those things, she is here feeding me, making sure my eight-months-pregnant body is comfortable as I sit and write, and offering her advice when I find myself getting stuck.

In many ways, this book is all about her, because I wouldn't be who I am without her. I wouldn't be able to write well without her teaching me to read as a child. I wouldn't know how to care about women if my mom hadn't demonstrated her care time and time again. And I wouldn't know God the way that I do if she had not continually pointed me back to Him.

Feminism has told us that motherhood is a prison that we must liberate ourselves from. But my mom has shown me the opposite is true. If I can impact even one person's life the way my mom has impacted mine, I will have lived a meaningful life.

This is the call of God for each of us as women. Regardless of whether or not you have children, you can mother like my mom has. You can lay your life down for others while expecting nothing in return. You can show others just how powerful God's love is by loving them powerfully. You can nurture souls by simply being present.

Far from the prison we are told it is, motherhood is the freedom to live a life of more significance than we will ever see come to fruition in our lifetime. Motherhood is the creation and nurturance of life itself.

JOURNALING:

- Consider the personal experiences and sacrifices your own mother or a mother figure in your life has made for you. What are the ways they have supported and nurtured you physically, spiritually, and emotionally? How has their love and presence impacted your life? Take a moment to express gratitude and appreciation to them for their role in your journey.

- Explore your beliefs and attitudes toward motherhood. How have societal narratives, including those promoted by feminism, shaped your perspective on motherhood? Reflect on the idea that motherhood can be a source of freedom, significance, and fulfill-ment. What are some ways you can embrace and celebrate the concept of motherhood, whether or not you have children?

DEEPER DIVE:

- Take a moment to talk to the Lord about any pain you have surrounding your relationship with your mom. Pour out your heart, inviting Him to heal the wounded places that have felt rejected or abandoned. Trust that His Holy Spirit brings comfort and restoration, wrapping you in His loving embrace.

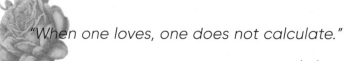

"When one loves, one does not calculate."

—THÉRÈSE DE LISIEUX

HOLY MARY, MOTHER OF GOD

In 2017, twenty-three-year-old me went to see *Wonder Woman* in theaters. I was moved to tears by the story of Diana, who had desires very similar to my own, but abilities far beyond what I could have imagined. She was kind, compassionate, and cared about the fate of those around her. Her passion for fighting injustice resonated with my own. She interacted with the world with childlike innocence, yet she seemed to have the wisdom of the sages.

Throughout the film, she offered her own subversive commentary on men and the ways they interact in the world. Hidden in plain sight was the feminist message again, and I ate it up. In my eyes, Diana was the moral image of what all women could be if men would just get out of the way and learn to be more like us.

I wanted to be just like her, so I made her my icon of womanhood. It didn't help my ego that my friends were regularly texting me to say, "I just saw *Wonder Woman*, and you look so much alike!" (This is still funny to me because I am far from athletic.) I dressed up like Wonder Woman at a university party, she was on my pageant vision board, and she even made an appearance in my final project for my degree in fashion.

As a fashion student, I spent a lot of time photoshopping pictures together. I used my photo editing skills to place Wonder Woman, Leslie Knope, and Olivia Culpo (my favorite Miss Universe) onto a pink background with phrases like "When I rise, we all rise!" I printed my collage out and taped it to the wall. I even made it the screensaver on my laptop.

While there is a lot to admire about Diana of Themyscira, she was not a real woman. She had magical powers, superhuman strength, and never aged. These qualities, I would argue, make her an incredibly unrealistic and, therefore, unhelpful role model. Looking back now, I also see how damaging her one-sided, holier-than-thou perspective on men was for a generation of women.

She became a tool of the "feminist spirit" to further spread the message that man = bad, stupid, and violent, and woman = sensitive, moralistic, and capable. Diana even argued that men were completely unnecessary for women outside of the need for their seed—a perspective that many feminists promote today. In the 2017 movie, she tells her love interest, Steve, "Men are essential for procreation, but when it comes to pleasure, unnecessary."

So why did I and so many other women develop an obsession with Wonder Woman? Her beauty, poise, and general badassery are clearly a few reasons, but I think it's also because the Christian world has failed to offer an alternative.

Growing up as a non-Catholic Christian, I found myself looking for biblical women who I could look up to, and there weren't a lot. While I love the description of the Proverbs 31 woman, I was tired of her being the one and only female that was talked about, with the exception of the occasional mention of Jael or Deborah—that is, until I started reading Catholic literature.

Suddenly, a biblical character who was often overlooked by my circle of Christianity came to life.

> Holy Mary, the Mother of God. Hail Mary, full of grace, the Lord is with thee. Blessed art thou among women, and blessed is the fruit of thy womb, Jesus.

This excerpt from the Hail Mary prayer is derived from her cousin Elizabeth's greeting when she arrived for a visit, after Mary had been told she would conceive Jesus.

Mary wasn't just a "birther" for a person who happened to become God. She was chosen by God to be the vessel that He would come into the world through. He could have beamed Himself down to earth Star Trek-style as a self-sufficient, all-knowing young man. But He didn't. God chose to come into the world through a woman, and not just any woman. He chose the young virgin, Mary.

When God announced His plans to bring our Savior into the world through her womb, her response quickly made it clear why she was chosen. An angelic being appeared to her—a teenage girl who had never been sexually intimate with a man—and told her that she was going to be pregnant. She didn't get angry, scared, or run away. Instead, she responded to the angel, "I am the servant of the Lord; let it be to me according to your word" (Luke 1:38).

This response is stunning! And I can't help but wonder how I would have responded.

As a pregnant mom myself, I can't imagine the swirl of emotions she was feeling. Pregnancy is not easy. Everything about your body changes. Your hormones have you simultaneously feeling every emotion known to man. And those first few months are typically filled with nausea and an otherworldly level of exhaustion.

For all believing women, Catholic or not, Mary is a real woman of wonder. She didn't have superhuman strength. When the Lord's messenger told her she would give birth, she knew this would be a vulnerable and likely painful experience. She was a righteous Jewish woman who knew the laws and knew the consequences of not following them. There was no guarantee that her miraculous conception would be accepted by the community or her fiancé.

Mary humbly responded to God's call with full surrender. The call was far from glamorous, brought judgment onto her, uprooted her life plans, and made her completely dependent on God and her future husband for her protection.

Unlike Diana, Mary wasn't a goddess; she was just a teenage girl. She really existed. She had to navigate life as a young wife and mother in an era before hospital births, parenting books, and the internet. She was truly an empowered woman because she walked in full surrender to God—not because she touted feminist slogans.

It isn't because of superhuman strength, physical beauty, or martial arts skills that Mary is admirable. Instead, it's her remarkable willingness to recognize that God's plans for her life would inevitably be better than her own. As the New Eve, she laid down her own ability to judge what is good and evil and allowed God to once again be seated as King over all that she was.

The idea that Mary is the New Eve comes from a Catholic idea that just as sin entered the world through the first woman, Eve, sin was erased from the world by Mary's surrender to God's plan. Eve leaned on her own understanding of good and evil and decided to disobey what God had spoken to her. In contrast, Mary fully surrendered her own plans for her life and said "yes" to God's plan of birthing the Savior through her. Mary is seen as a new and improved Eve who, through her obedience to God and her willingness to bear the Savior of the world, undid the damage caused by the disobedience of the first woman.

The popularity of movies like *Wonder Woman* makes it clear that women today need strong role models to look to for direction and to imitate on the path of life. We can look to Mary as an example of exactly what is required of us in its simplest form—surrender to the plans that our Father has for us.

As I prepare for the delivery of my own son, I can imagine to some degree how Mary might have been feeling. There is a deep connection that you experience with your unborn child, especially once you feel them move. But there is also so much unknown. How will his birth be? Will I be a good mother? Will my baby like me? Will my body ever feel like mine again? And about a million other questions.

Mary was pregnant in a literal sense with Jesus, but also in a metaphorical sense with God's promise of purpose and fulfillment. Each of us is invited by God to do the same—to make our bodies and our spirits vessels to carry and grow His promises in. This walk with Him is not without questions and concerns, but we continue on regardless. Like Mary, we have the opportunity to say, "May it be to me according to Your will." We can partner with the same spirit of surrender that Mary had and lay down our personal opinions about what is good and bad for our lives, allowing Him to define our success and fruitfulness.

I've found that a great way to kickstart a new level of surrender to the Lord is to simply tell Him you want to surrender. For me, it typically goes something like, "Father, _____ is what I want out of life. These are my plans and what I think is best. I surrender all of these hopes and plans to you. Guide me and help me see where You are leading me, whether it includes my plans or not."

There is always a sense of peace that accompanies these moments of recognizing my humanity and inability to see how my life fits into the bigger picture. I offer the steering wheel of my life back to the One who sees it all. Sometimes He directs me on the path I was expecting, and at other times He pivots things. Either way, I find joy in knowing that I have at least attempted to let go of my need to control things.

Romans 8:28 says, "And we know that for those who love God all things work together for good, for those who are called according to his purpose." This verse is not a promise that God is always working to make people's lives easier and happier. It is a promise that when we walk in surrender to Him, He is working to bring fulfillment and redemption to even the difficult paths we will walk.

This scripture has been a constant encouragement to me in my own journey of surrender. I may not be in "control" of my life (who really is, anyway?), but the One who is in control is on a mission to bring forth good fruit from my life. Through my surrender, He is nurturing and growing a promise that He will birth through my life. That is a beautiful promise.

JOURNALING:

- Take a moment to surrender, sister. Are there areas where you struggle to let go of control and trust in God's plans and timing? How might embracing surrender bring more peace and fulfillment to your life? Tell the Lord, "Let it be to me according to Your will."

- Who are some women, real or fictional, that you admire and look up to? What qualities do they possess that you find inspiring or empowering?

- Journal about your own journey of womanhood. How have you grown and evolved over time in understanding your femininity? Are there specific moments or decisions that have shaped your understanding of yourself as a woman or as an individual?

IF WOMEN ARE VICTIMS, THEN EVERYONE IS

I was recently watching an interview with Dr. Jordan Peterson where a feminist was pressing him on why he did not accept the premise of women's oppression—even before we had the right to vote or own our own bank account. He pointed out a truth that was eye-opening for me.

Life wasn't good for anyone until recently—male or female. Arguably, life still isn't that great for most people. It's only now that a select minority of us living in developed nations have become so comparatively fortunate thanks to wealth, technology, and medical advancement that we even have the time to consider ideas like feminism.

For all of human history, humans have suffered greatly—from disease, war, and famine, to name a few reasons. Men suffered from these things just as much as women did, but often to a greater degree as their social status typically obligated them to take greater risks in all areas of life in order to protect their wives and children.

This is not to say that women didn't have their own unique challenges and hardships, but to merely point out that men did as well. We talk about men in history as if they were all living like kings and women existed as their sexual slaves, but it is safe to say that almost none of us would prefer to be a man 100, 200, 500, or 1,000 years ago instead of a woman today.

It is good to study history with an eye to the future. In fact, I would say it's necessary to learn from our past to avoid repeating it. But in doing so, we must be careful not to victimize ourselves and vil-

lainize men. Both men and women faced horrible realities throughout history that I would never wish to live out. Sometimes those realities were harder on women, and sometimes on men.

Life is still hard for everyone. Although we live longer and have
a higher quality of life than any other generation in history, there are
massive challenges that we face as women that men do not face. However, men also face significant challenges that we are unaware of and
cannot be fully aware of because we aren't them.

As I shared in Chapter 1, I struggled for 10 years with undiagnosed
endometriosis—a debilitating disease that significantly impacts the
lives of at least 10 percent of women globally.[2] I've seen this disease
wreck lives with the constant pain, hospital visits, and infertility that
often accompany it. I want to be very careful how I talk about this because the destruction that endometriosis creates in the lives of women
is very real. Many women who suffer from endometriosis end up taking
their own lives because of the torment it can bring. It is for this very
reason that I believe it is extremely important to present a different
way of facing our own suffering. Endometriosis and every other kind of
suffering will exist until Jesus returns, and I don't want to see another
life stolen by these inescapable difficulties.

By college, my endometriosis flares had sadly become a normal, yet
still very traumatic, part of my life. My first bad flare came on while I
was competing in a local pageant. I woke up with what I thought were
"normal" cramps, but the pain only got worse.

I sat in a hot dressing room with fifty other women, gritting my
teeth in pain as I teased my hair. I stood up, and the room started to
spin, but I was determined to compete. I collected my wardrobe and
crawled up the stairs to the stage wings.

[2]The World Endometriosis Research Foundation, "Facts About Endometriosis." Endometriosis.org, https://endometriosis.org/resources/articles/facts-about-endometriosis/.

"Justice Enlow! Twenty-four, the Fashion Institute of Design and Merchandising!" I was able to yell into the mic before scrambling backstage and collapsing. My mom rushed to my side, helped me stumble to the car, and we quickly drove to the emergency room.

Another particularly horrible flare began when I was at home a few months later. I was sitting on my bedroom floor working on homework when the pain hit. I struggled down the stairs to where my parents were in the living room and told them what was happening.

My mom encouraged me to sit on the sofa and rest in an attempt to hold off the flare. It didn't help. It was a searing, twisting pain in my lower abdomen and pelvic floor. It felt like I was sitting on fire while being stabbed with a hot iron in the stomach.

I progressed from tears to screaming, "Please call an ambulance!" as if going back to the ER and being given more morphine was the solution. My parents tried to pick me up and carry me to the bathtub to ease the pain, but being touched while experiencing so much pain was too much. My body started shaking, and I couldn't see from the intensity.

My mom forced a pain pill into my mouth as I writhed, waiting for it to kick in. Roughly a half hour later, the medicine started working and took the edge off.

This flare, like the rest of them, took me days to recover from. The pain was so severe, even with the medication, that I couldn't get out of bed for a few more days. We weren't sure what exactly was causing the pain, but we knew it was connected to my period. After a three-day hospital stay, even the doctors didn't know how to help. I finally decided I would have to be the one to diagnose myself. I spent a few months reading everything I could about others who were experiencing similar pain. Endometriosis kept coming up, so I figured this was my diagnosis.

I have seen women who have responded to this diagnosis in two very different ways. One response is to say things like, "My body hates me," and "My uterus is trying to kill me." This perspective ends up spilling over into other areas of life too. Endometriosis and chronic illness become the defining identity of this woman. She is sucked into the pit of hopelessness.

I have seen other women respond by determining endometriosis would not become their defining identity. Instead of using endometriosis as a scapegoat for their disappointments in life, they used their struggle to propel themselves forward. When I saw this, I was inspired to do the same. My day-to-day reality was very much the same as the women who were victimized by endometriosis, but I refused to see myself as a victim.

While resting and caring for my body when my endometriosis would flare up, I allowed the pain to refine me and motivate me to help others. I didn't want endometriosis to win. Pain would not be my god. Driven by that same childhood desire to help women, I refused to surrender, and I knew if I could figure out a solution, it would help other women who were also suffering.

I created a nonprofit organization that helped educate other women on endometriosis so that they could have answers and a diagnosis sooner than I had. When I had my surgery, I spent my recovery telling everyone I could about this life-changing option. The surgery that I had—wide excision instead of ablation—is only familiar to a minority of endo sufferers. That needed to change. Helping other women is what helped me keep my mind out of victimhood.

I truly believe that my hope in the face of those dark years helped me get to where I am today. I haven't suffered from any symptoms of endometriosis since my surgery, almost five years ago. As for the infertility that can often accompany endometriosis, as you know, I am currently eight months pregnant with my own miracle.

Now, I am not trying to promise you that having a positive outlook is going to make your life easy. But I will say that allowing yourself to become hopeless and nihilistic in response to the real challenges of life will absolutely kill you.

Regardless of whether or not the specific challenge you face is endometriosis, the principle remains the same: The hope we have in God is the only dependable light through the dark night of our souls. He doesn't need you to be healthy, wealthy, or a genius to accomplish His purpose for you. He simply needs you to make the most of what you have been given and to be willing to serve.

Moses struggled with his speech but went on to lead the entire nation of Israel to freedom from slavery; Deborah was a woman judge in a patriarchal society; David was literally hunted by his father-in-law but became the king of Israel and the ancestor of Jesus; Jesus was hated but redeemed all of humanity from sin. Far from these struggles preventing these biblical characters from accomplishing what God had placed within them, the difficulties they faced actually made their stories more incredible.

When I am in a season of struggling, I like to read the psalms. David did an incredible job of honestly communicating his emotional despair. He did not positive-think his way out of the very real struggles he faced. He instead took them to God as he poured out his heart before Him. He questioned God honestly but he always came back around to praising Him.

Reading the psalms is an amazing psychological exercise in releasing your pain and suffering to God and then reminding your soul of His presence and promise over your life.

I genuinely love the fact that our generation can openly talk about mental health and therapy. I have worked with a therapist in the past to help me process the pain and struggles I've experienced in life, and I highly recommend it for when you find yourself emotionally stuck.

However, if your therapy and mental healing journey doesn't eventually help you reconnect with truth outside of your feelings and experiences, something needs to change. All too often, I hear people use their therapist as an excuse to worship their feelings. I have found therapy most beneficial when my counselor helps me determine which of my feelings are based in reality and which are not.

Our feelings and emotions are a gift from God and certainly point to a part of His nature that we carry. Feelings are not evil, as some fundamentalist groups would have us believe. But our feelings are also not innately good, helpful, or true. Every feeling must be taken to the Lord to help us analyze it honestly. It's when we have a distorted perspective of God—that He hates our feelings and needs to process them—that we are hindered in our ability to do this.

Becoming an empowered woman requires us to stop allowing our limitations to define us and start letting God define us. He didn't place His image and His Holy Spirit inside of us so that we would roll over and surrender when we face our unique female challenges. We are not victims of our periods, our fertility, our motherhood, our hormones, our emotions, our fathers and husbands (unless they are abusive, in which case it is very important that you get away from them), or our friendships. Our fertility and motherhood are gifts that we are given and gifts that we then get to offer back to the Lord. The way we honor our fathers is a gift to both ourselves and our fathers. The way we love and respect our husbands is a gift to them that then is given back to us.

Far from the victimhood status feminism has claimed for us, God has claimed victory for us. We can no longer let society define what is good and evil. Our God has said that our femininity and the many different challenges that come along with it are good. That can be enough!

JOURNALING

How has your relationship with God influenced your response to suffering? Have
you found solace or guidance in knowing
that Jesus also experienced suffering? How
can you find contentment in suffering while also having faith
for redemption in your situation?

_____

_____

_____

_____

_____

_____

_____

_____

_____

_____

_____

_____

When things get rough, seeking help is brave! Have you reached out to therapists, counselors, or support groups during challenging periods? How did God's love shine through them and contribute to your healing?

_____

_____

_____

_____

_____

_____

_____

_____

_____

_____

_____

_____

_____

_____

Think back to those moments when you showed incredible strength and resilience. What helped you bounce back? How can you cultivate that inner warrior to face any future battles with confidence?

_____

_____

_____

_____

_____

_____

_____

_____

_____

_____

_____

_____

_____

_____

Gratitude is a game-changer! Reflect on the things you're thankful for, even during the toughest times. How does gratitude shift your perspective from victimhood to a place of empowerment? Let's celebrate the little victories together!

CHAPTER 6

CREATED FOR FRUITFULNESS

"[T]HE DESIRE FOR FRUITFULNESS, HOWEVER CULTURALLY FOREIGN AND CLUMSILY ARTICULATED, REMAINS A DESIRE SEWN INTO THE SOUL OF WOMEN AND WILL EVENTUALLY FIND A WAY TO EXPRESS ITSELF IN ONE FORM OR ANOTHER."

—CARRIE GRESS & NOELLE MERRING,
Theology of the Home I

WE ARE ALL MOTHERS

As I've mentioned, my parents pastored a non-denominational charismatic church for most of my childhood. This means my early memories are peppered with flag ladies, shofars, and fire tunnels (if you don't know what that is, imagine a conga line where people yell at you in tongues). We were about as far from orthodox Christianity as you can be while still being Christians.

I loved a lot of the dynamics that this spiritual upbringing brought into my life. A common phrase that was repeated by adults was, "There is no junior Holy Spirit!" This meant my personal relationship with God was taken seriously from the beginning. We were taught to pray for miracles, prophesy, and worship God with freedom of expression. My parents took me on ministry trips all over the world where I met many other people who believed similarly to us. There was a deep understanding that anything natural or supernatural was possible for God.

The downside of our unorthodox beliefs was that, inevitably, some important things were unintentionally skipped over for the sake of preserving freedom. Charismatics don't like rules, to a fault, as they are often seen as boxes that we are placing God in. This means the only unifying principle in the charismatic movement is that the Holy Spirit is still alive and active today. That leaves a whole lot of room for questions about everything else in life, and the answers people come up with are as colorful as the flags they were waving at church.

I am extremely thankful for my spiritual upbringing because it gave me the most important things: a relationship with God through Jesus and an active relationship with the Holy Spirit, without saying too much about anything else. This perspective might offend charismatics or even some of the people I grew up in church with. This is not my intention at all, but I don't mind criticizing some of the weaknesses of a movement that I know intimately.

Unlike those who experienced trauma and spiritual abuse at the hands of a specific denomination, I have had an openness to the truthful perspectives on God that I am sure other denominations have tapped into. I was never hurt by the Baptist, Catholic, or Pentecostal Church, so it is easy for me to learn from the truth they have faithfully protected about the nature of God while spitting out the "seeds" of less helpful information.

One of the topics that the Catholic Church has undoubtedly excelled in is how they view women. As an outsider, my perspective is that they have arrived at this conclusion because of the high position of honor that they give to Mary, the mother of Jesus. Her role as the "New Eve" means that she is seen by Catholics as an ideal that all women can strive for. She is the archetypical example of what a woman of God can be. Because of this, Catholic women view their position in the Kingdom of God with significance—working to become more like Mary, a woman fully surrendered to God.

In addition to the influence Mary has had on their perspective of women, Pope John Paul II shared a series of messages during his time as Pope that have since been compiled into a doctrine called *Theology of the Body*. I discovered *Theology of the Body* a few years ago and was immediately impacted by it. I had been searching for a scriptural teaching about the significance of our human bodies, our sexuality, and God's intentionality in bringing together men and women in marriage. My perspective on the fruitfulness of women has been heavily influenced by Catholic teaching and *Theology of the Body*.

But back to my story. In high school, I found myself searching for teachings about what it meant to be a godly woman. At the time, almost nothing existed from a charismatic perspective, and the resources that did exist were vague and lacked practical life application. In my search, I stumbled across blogs written by other women my age who were very zealous for the Lord. These fellow homeschoolers, who probably only had fifteen people reading their posts, including me, loved reading Scripture and seeking how to apply it to daily life in practical ways. Somehow, while maintaining my junior feminist worldview, I also began to adopt the fundamentalist Baptist views of the young women I was reading online.

At thirteen or fourteen years old, I stopped watching most TV, listening to non-Christian music, and started dressing very modestly. We're talking long-denim-skirts-level modesty. And while I don't think this phase lasted for more than a year, my desire for answers about how to live radically for God as a woman continued. Because I didn't find answers in the church, I sought to define my identity as a woman of God using feminist theory applied to Scripture.

After my feminist deconstruction, I was looking for helpful teachings about marriage, men, and women as I was preparing for my own marriage. Through social media, I met a sweet Catholic girl who was around my age and had recently been married herself. She told me about the teaching of *Theology of the Body*, and it immediately caught my interest.

This wasn't the shallow women's ministry content that I had grown up with. It also wasn't the subjugation to second-class citizenship in the Kingdom that I had learned from my fundamentalist bloggers. As a non-denominational Christian, I was excited to have found answers to the longing of my heart, and shocked that they came from the Catholic Church.

JOURNALING:

- Let's dive into the meaning of having a personal relationship with God. Do you feel that closeness with Him? How can you deepen that connection even more? Remember, He's always there, eager to embrace you!

- Rules and guidelines in religious practices can be a dance, right? How do you personally navigate the tension between freedom and structure in your spiritual life? Are there any areas where finding that sweet spot gets a bit challenging?

- How do you currently perceive and embrace your femininity? Are there any natural tendencies or aspects of your femininity that you would like to cultivate and grow? How can you experience more of God's love and intentionality in creating you as a woman?

DEEPER DIVE:

- Take some time to research different faith traditions and their perspectives on women. How are women seen in Catholicism, Calvanism, Pentecostalism, Orthodoxy, etc.? What do you agree and disagree with? What scriptures inform your perspective?

LESS-IDEAL SEASONS

We exist at an interesting time in history. In many ways, the world is a better place than it's ever been, with more access to clean drinking water, medical technology, a greater understanding of hygiene, and unlimited information available at our fingertips thanks to the Internet.

At the same time, we've created a world that moves so quickly and depends so much on efficiency that it often leaves no room for our needs as humans with souls. I believe that God has solutions for these problems that we have created for ourselves, and He wants to involve us in the process of healing culture.

In the meantime, each of us still has to live in the world as it exists now. Most women will have to have jobs in workplaces that do not consider our unique needs. We still have to use public restrooms that don't provide a changing table for our babies. We still get looks when our young children have meltdowns in public.

I believe that both Scripture and our bodies testify to a man's position as the provider in the home and a woman's call to focus on cultivating a home that supports her husband in this role, especially during the developmental years of the lives of their children.

However, this ideal is not possible for everyone. There are seasons when what makes the most sense for your family is you working and your husband staying home with the kids. Sometimes both you and your husband might need to work.

You might feel shocked at how old-fashioned this sounds. But there are many women who desire to stay home and care for their families, but for whatever reason, they cannot and find themselves facing profound disappointment because of it. If that is you, remember that this season doesn't have to last forever.

It is important to continue taking this desire to the Lord. He ingrained you with a desire to be there for your family, and He will not leave you without an opportunity to express that part of your femininity. In the meantime, intentionally cultivate other ways of manifesting your femininity and honoring your husband as the leader of your family. This will take a ton of grace for yourself and forgiveness toward God and your husband.

JOURNALING:

- God has solutions for the problems we have and desires to involve us in the process of healing culture! What is your role in contributing to positive change and bringing healing to the world around you?

- Dream with me, sister! How can your world adapt to better meet your unique needs as a woman? More flexible working hours, paid maternity leave, or something else? Your desires matter, so let's explore ways to bring them to life!

- Are there ways you can cultivate and honor your femininity, even in the absence of certain circumstances or opportunities?

GENESIS

At the beginning of time, God bestowed humanity with a mandate for fruitfulness and dominion. This fruitfulness looks different for men and women, and it is an ancient call on our lives. After disobeying

God and eating the fruit of the tree of the knowledge of good and evil, man and woman had their eyes opened to judging good and evil for the first time.

The immediate result of their disobedience was that they started judging good and bad, and coming to different conclusions than God did. When God created them and placed them in the garden naked, He said it was good. But Adam and Eve, now ashamed of their nakedness, judged that being naked in the Garden was not good. This was just the beginning of the process of humans placing their judgment above God's—not because we hate God, but because of fear and shame.

What God spoke to them following their disobedience has often been called a curse. However, Dr. Jordan Peterson points out that when God speaks to Adam and Eve after they have sinned, He is describing the natural consequences of self-awareness and not giving punishment.[1] You don't have to agree with me on this point, but I think it has some interesting potential implications.

Life in the Garden was a paradise before sin had its stronghold on human hearts. We walked in intimacy with each other and with God. There was no shame in our nakedness because there was no self-awareness that comes with our ability to judge what is good and not good. We were naked and unashamed because we trusted God when He said, "It is good." We accepted His gifts and designs as good because He said they were.

If the "curse" can be read as a description of what naturally happens when our eyes are opened to good and evil—a consequence of self-awareness—then we can reason that God is identifying the different ways self-awareness affects women vs. men when He says the following:

---

[1] Jordan Peterson, *12 Rules for Life: An Antidote to Chaos* (Toronto: Random House Canada, 2018).

To the woman He said,

"I will greatly multiply
Your pain in childbirth,
In pain you shall deliver children;
Yet your desire will be for your husband,
And he shall rule over you."

Then to Adam He said, "Because you have listened to the voice of your wife, and have eaten from the tree about which I commanded you, saying, 'You shall not eat from it';

Cursed is the ground because of you;
With hard labor you shall eat from it
All the days of your life.
Both thorns and thistles it shall grow for you;
Yet you shall eat the plants of the field;
By the sweat of your face
You shall eat bread,
Until you return to the ground,
Because from it you were taken;
For you are dust,
And to dust you shall return."

—GENESIS 3:16–19 NASB

Now that their eyes are open, the woman can see her own vulnerability and her need for male protection. This makes her aware of her need for her husband. Man is now aware that he and his wife are vulnerable to death and that he must do something about it. He wonders if one day God's provision for them will end, and they will starve.

He begins to be burdened with his need to plan ahead and be prepared to keep himself and his new wife alive, a task he will accomplish through toiling and striving against the ground. This is the price of sin. This is the cost of making a god out of ourselves and our own judgment.

Positioning ourselves as the judge of right and wrong is still something that every single one of us is guilty of. We often reject God's definitions of right and wrong, male and female, life-giving and death-giving, in exchange for what culture tells us.

It's important that we realize that the differences in men and women, from our bodies to our spirits, are not a consequence of sin. These differences existed in paradise, before sin came. Rather, the consequences of sin point to the original design of men and women as very different but complementary creatures.

Because men and women are innately different, the way sin and self-awareness affect them is different. Even in our perfect state, before sin, we were different.

God's first remedy to humanity's predicament is to gift them with a set of rules that will help them exist under the framework of trusting Him once again, starting with the paramount rule, "You shall have no other gods before Me."

This includes making ourselves gods! I see the gift of the Ten Commandments and the Law of Moses (called the Torah) to His chosen people as a way of helping man overcome his own awareness of good and evil and once again depend on God.

Reading through the Old Testament, we see that humans continued to struggle with this surrender. Instead of God's rules bringing life to the Israelites, they found themselves again applying their own understanding of good and evil to the process of living out God's law. They even added to what He spoke to them.

God's solution was to send His Son and His Holy Spirit to teach us how to walk in surrender to Him and His commands. Jesus continually modeled for us what surrendering our own judgment—our perception of good and evil—and leaning on the will of our heavenly Father looks like.

After Jesus ascended back into heaven, He sent His Holy Spirit to dwell in each of us. This Spirit guides and convicts us if we allow Him to. He is a constant helper in our journey toward overcoming self-defined perceptions of good and evil in favor of God-defined ones.

The law filtered through our humanistic perspectives on good and evil brought death, but by the power and guidance of the Holy Spirit and the freedom purchased for us by the death and resurrection of Jesus, we can again pursue living according to God's commands in a way that brings life. Through the grace of Jesus, we can once again remove ourselves as our own personal gods and learn to surrender to the judgment of our Father God.

In *Theology of the Body*, Pope John Paul II points out that everything God created in the Garden was good. The first time God notices that something is not good is when He sees that man is alone. However, there is no animal in the Garden that is suitable for companionship with man (shockingly, not even a dog).

This is because only man was created in the image of God. Only man is body and spirit—the body giving form and expression to his spiritual reality.

"Man is part of the natural world, but, at the same time, he is set apart from it. He isn't like the other animals—he alone is made in God's likeness. That's why he's given stewardship over the earth. This also explains why man cannot be defined in purely naturalistic or materialistic terms. Yes, man is a physical being. But already, on the first page of the Bible, we learn that man can't be explained as a merely physical being—a collection of cells, tissues, and organs. Human beings transcend the categories of chemistry and biology. Ultimately, man can only be understood in relation to God. This great mystery of creation—that we are created in God's image—is the key reference point for understanding all aspects of humanity, including our sexuality."[2]

We can begin to find more clarity on what it means to live as a woman of God when we recognize two fundamental truths: We only find our identity as spiritual beings in relation to God, and as feminine beings in relation to man. Much to the disappointment of the feminist spirit, we cannot understand our femininity without understanding men's masculinity. We also cannot understand our own spiritual existence without understanding God—both realities that will always contain elements of mystery.

All of this is important because many feminist Christians have tried to argue that the differences between men and women are a consequence of the "curse" and are therefore something that we do not need to live in "subjugation to" now that Jesus paid the price. If this was the case, men and women would have had no distinctions before sin, and therefore, the consequences of sin in the world would have affected both in the same way.

While there are countless perspectives on exactly what Jesus's death provided beyond eternal life, it is clear that a blanket reversal of Eden did not happen. Men still have to work to eat. Thorns and thistles still grow. And much to my disappointment, women still experience pain in childbirth.

Fruitfulness in our lives must again be surrendered to God and His perspective of us. Understanding our unique role in fruitfulness as women requires us to look at the guideposts God originally gave us: our

---

[2]Pope John Paul II, *Theology of the Body in Simple Language*, (Philokalia Books, 2009).

bodies, our spirits, and our understanding of our male counterparts. Each of these things plays a role in helping us orient ourselves to our original design as carriers of God's feminine image.

To successfully walk out our mandate as women of God, we must seek to replace our self-awareness with God-awareness, self-dependence with God-dependence, and self-defined femininity with God-defined femininity. This process takes intentionality and surrender. We must come to our Father and His Word with an openness to having our lives and our worldviews turned upside down.

JOURNALING:

- Reflect on the concept of self-awareness and the ability to judge good and evil. How have you experienced the consequences of self-awareness in your own life? Have there been instances where your judgments differed from God's perspective? How can you cultivate a humble heart that embraces God's wisdom above your own?

- In what ways do you find the consequences of self-awareness affecting men and women differently?

- Are there areas of your life where you tend to rely on cultural definitions rather than seeking God's guidance?

DEEPER DIVE

- In Genesis we read that the differences between men and women existed in paradise before sin. How does this perspective challenge or confirm your understanding of gender distinctions?

- Let's take a moment to sit with Father God. Ask Him how He sees your femininity. Ask Him to help you honor the distinctions between men and women that He created at the beginning of time.

OUR BODIES AS A TESTIMONY OF HIS PURPOSE

There's an interesting perspective that I have often heard in Christian circles. It's one that trivializes the physical world and overemphasizes the supernatural. And while it's obviously important that we remember these bodies and this world are not our eternal home, it's also important that we embrace the physical world we currently exist in.

If God decided it was important to give us physical bodies before sin even entered the world, then our bodies must be important. Our bodies are a physical manifestation of our spirits. Our physical existence is in no way trivial. We were, after all, created in the image of God. That means the physical and spiritual are both essential parts of what makes us who we are.

Pope John Paul II described our bodies as sacramental, as they make the invisible visible. Our bodies give form to us—not just to the obvious parts of us like our genetics and heritage, but also to our very spirits. Not only that, but our bodies are a dwelling place for the Spirit of God. 1 Corinthians 6:19 says, "[Y]our body is a temple of the Holy Spirit within you, whom you have from God . . ."

Understanding this reality reminds us that our bodies can teach us many lessons about how God created us to function spiritually. As women, we are fitted with a womb to carry and grow new life in. We have breasts that feed and nourish the most vulnerable—our infants. Even our arm joints were crafted in such a way that carrying our children is more natural for us than for men.[3]

There is an obvious, natural conclusion we can draw from these facts: God has designed us to be biological mothers. But there is also a

---

[3]Rakesh Kumar Adhikari, Subodh Kumar Yadav, and Abhishek Karn, "A Comparative Study of Carrying Angle with Respect to Sex and Dominant Arm in Eastern Population of Nepal," *International Journal of Current Research and Review* 9, no. 7 (April 2017): 19-22, https://www.researchgate.net/publication/316853394_A_comparative_study_of_carrying_angle_with_respect_to_sex_and_dominant_arm_in_eastern_population_of_Nepal.

spiritual reality revealed through our physical formation. Saint Edith Stein wrote, "The woman's soul is fashioned as a shelter in which other souls may unfold."[4] This is a beautiful description of the way we were created to function as women. This is not a limitation on what we do; rather, it is a description of how God created us to function.

Sadly, by advancing the feminist agenda, we have given up our very right to manifest feminine fruitfulness. We are encouraged to delay having children until we have been "productive" enough in our careers. We work jobs for businesses that do the bare minimum to support our womanhood. Rather than acknowledge and accommodate our unique hormone cycles, we are instead encouraged to display our fruitfulness in a masculine way. In order to function in Western nations, it is almost a requirement that we take some form of birth control. There is no room for the inefficiency of our changing physical needs associated with having a period or a potential "unplanned" pregnancy.

Masculine fruitfulness is about provision and protection. Man's biology makes this clear. Productivity and efficiency are high on the masculinity value hierarchy. And speaking of hierarchy, men naturally gravitate toward and excel in hierarchical settings, whereas women typically prefer to maintain more egalitarian relationships with one another.[5] But there is no room for the egalitarian dynamic when competition is the only way to succeed.[6] Consequently, women must develop masculine traits in order to climb the corporate ladder.

[4]Edith Stein, "Principles of Women's Education," Kolbe Foundation, August 14, 1999, https://www.kolbefoundation.org/gbookswebsite/studentlibrary/greatestbooks/aaabooks/stein/principleswomeneducation.html.
[5]Jordan Peterson, *12 Rules for Life: An Antidote to Chaos* (Toronto: Random House Canada, 2018).
[6]Merriam-Webster. "Egalitarianism: a social philosophy advocating the removal of inewualities among people" Merriam-Webster.com Dictionary, Merriam-Webster, https://www.merriam-webster.com/dictionary/egalitarianism. Accessed July 12, 2023.

"Culture derives from woman—for had she not taught her children to talk, the great spiritual values of the world would not have passed from generation to generation. After nourishing the substance of the body to which she gave birth, she then nourishes the child with the substance of her mind. As guardian of the values of the spirit, as protectress of the morality of the young, she preserves culture, which deals with purposes and ends, while man upholds civilization, which deals only with means."[7]

To generalize, masculinity can be seen as the machine and femininity as the soul. Both are valuable. Both are strong. Both are irrelevant without the other. The more mechanical and practical fruitfulness that men are created for is different from the emotional and soul-developing fruitfulness of women.

I'm not going to propose a solution to this problem, because your solution will largely depend on if you think it's ideal for women to have careers outside the home. As someone who prefers to stay in the philosophical, I don't know if it's possible for large businesses to make the necessary accommodations to help women manifest their femininity in the workplace in a way that wouldn't financially hurt the company.

Currently, the average workplace does not nurture the needs of most women. Regardless of any future changes that might take place to make working conditions more hospitable for us, because the cost of living is so much higher today than it was for our parents and grandparents, most of us have to find ways to function in jobs and careers that are not suited to our feminine needs.

If you aren't thriving in your corporate job, it's probably because it wasn't created to suit your needs. Instead of using this information to

[7]Fulton John Sheen, *World's First Love: Mary, Mother of God* (San Francisco: Ignatius Press, 2009), 184, 185.

fuel your hatred of men (who often thrive in corporate environments), allow it to help you be more compassionate toward yourself.

If our society revolved around women's fruitfulness, we would never judge our male counterparts for being unable to grow new humans and give birth to them. Don't do the equivalent to yourself as you find ways to still succeed in your workplace.

I think a place we can clearly see the need for more feminine-friendly jobs is in the multi-level marketing industry. Love them or hate them, MLMs appeal to our need for careers that allow us to manifest our femininity through our work. They also provide women with female mentors and flexible working hours that allow them to prioritize their families over their jobs.

Maybe someday there will be a viable way to run businesses that is ideal for the needs of women and also doesn't come at the cost of forcing men to adopt feminine roles in companies. A redemptive aspect of the COVID-19 pandemic was that families were finally able to integrate working life with home life. Businesses found ways to facilitate working from home, which enabled parents to have more time with their kids. Kids were doing school at home and getting more one-on-one help than is often available in a traditional school setting.

JOURNALING:

- How do you experience the interplay between your body and spirit? Have you overemphasized either your physical or spiritual existence?

- Our bodies are temples of the Holy Spirit. Take a moment to ponder how this profound truth shapes your perspective on caring for and honoring your physical vessel. How can you cultivate a deeper connection between your physical and spiritual well-being?

THE ATTACK ON OUR FERTILITY

We can express our fruitfulness in almost everything that we do as women, but the clearest expression of this fruitfulness is motherhood. This motherhood will be manifest in a literal sense by most of us, but spiritual motherhood is also available to us all.

Just as our physical womb is a place where new life is formed, fed, and grown, we can spiritually mother others in a similar manner. Our spirit can act as a womb in which the lives of others can take shelter, be fed spiritual food, and grow into mature spiritual beings. The mystery of a spiritual motherhood is reflected in the mystery of our physical motherhood.

I am currently eight months pregnant, and without modern technology, I would have no knowledge that my baby is a boy. My physical body has changed drastically in order to safely harbor his precious little body. Yet, even with all the obvious changes, there is so much mystery. He is so real to me, yet in a very different way than the people I can see around me. In many ways, pregnancy is a surreal feeling, but simultaneously the most real.

Often our spiritual motherhood reflects these same realities. We are mothering a person, a movement, a message that God has placed into our spiritual womb. It isn't quite clear to us what is growing, only that something is there.

It is clear from the design of our physical bodies that all of us were created for motherhood, regardless of whether we have biological children. While I believe that physical motherhood is a calling for the majority of women, I would be remiss in not acknowledging the many women called to motherhood in other capacities. Infertility and God-ordained singleness are two obvious situations where biological motherhood is not the manifestation of fruitfulness. But these circumstances do not mean that your call to motherhood is any less legitimate!

Catholic philosopher Alice von Hildebrand, childless herself, beautifully illustrated this point when she wrote, "Motherhood is not only biological maternity. It is spiritual maternity. There are hundreds of people all around who are desperately looking for a mother . . . I totally reject the idea that you are not a mother unless you have children of your own . . . From now on your daily prayer should be, 'God, send me spiritual children and I will never turn any one of them down. The more the better.' Simple as that. Pray for the gift of spiritual children. It might very well be that in your beautiful desire to be a biological mother you have overlooked cases where you could have become a spiritual mother."[8]

The pain of longing for biological children and having no control over your fulfillment seems to be one of the greatest pains a woman can face. Whether it's because of an inability to conceive and carry a child or the unmet desire for a husband, our desire for fruitfulness is deeply ingrained in each of us.

I cannot pretend to understand the pain that accompanies both of these circumstances, but I am thankful for a God who has given us a way to manifest that part of our identity regardless. In a world full of broken and hurting people, you have been called to shelter and nurture the souls of others. You have been called to allow your very body to be sacrificed for the nurturance of who God has called you to.

Unsurprisingly, our call to motherhood is clearly seen as a hindrance to the feminist "utopia," and many so-called solutions have been suggested. Feminist thought leader Sophie Lewis has proposed mass surrogacy as the solution. Reproduction would be a career that "gestators" function in, and children would be shared by the collective community.[9]

Scientists have proposed an artificial womb as a potential future "solution" to motherhood. Baby farms could have thousands of EctoLife

---

[8]Alice von Hildebrand, "Spiritual Motherhood: Every Woman's Calling," *Plough*, May 8, 2022, https://www.plough.com/en/topics/life/parenting/spiritual-motherhood.
[9]Sophie Lewis, *Full Surrogacy Now: Feminism Against Family* (New York: Verso, 2019).

pods where parents would grow their children—making pregnancy and childbirth a thing of the past.

These are just a few of the ideas that people have come up with as they play god with all aspects of human existence. As in the Garden, these people, no doubt inspired by many feminist claims, have determined that God's design of fruitfulness is not good.

As our physical motherhood has been attacked, so too has our spiritual motherhood. The idea of laying our lives down for another, giving our bodies to nurture the soul of another, is seen as the type of relationship that distracts us from the ultimate goal—career success. Spiritual motherhood lacks the glamour and social prestige that characterizes the valued achievements of today's society.

Another example of our inability to rely on God's definition of good and evil for our fruitfulness is the issue of abortion. Early feminists claimed that women would never truly be liberated without contraception and abortion (for when contraception fails). Today's feminists have kept the torch lit as they continue to chant "My body, my choice!" at every Women's March.

What is silently communicated to us about our motherhood as cries for "abortion on demand" and baby farms reach our ears? Our motherhood is, at best, an unnecessary waste of time, and, at worst, a complete hindrance to us being successful women. If we can farm out the role of growing and nurturing our infants, then choosing to carry your own baby will be seen as a romantic and impractical notion. And abortion makes women who choose pregnancy seem irresponsible if the pregnancy is the least bit inconvenient to their career and life goals.

The attack on our fruitfulness is not limited to abortion and machine surrogacy. Miscarriage and infertility rates in women have also been steadily increasing since the women's liberation movement of the

1960s,[10] and waiting to begin having children in our 30s when fertility is naturally lower has also increased in popularity.

JOURNALING:

- Reflect on the concept of spiritual motherhood and how it relates to your own life. How have you experienced the nurturing and support of others, or perhaps even acted as a spiritual mother to someone else? How does this form of motherhood differ from biological motherhood?

- Sister, I understand that the topic of motherhood can sometimes evoke pain and deep emotions. If you carry any wounds or unfulfilled desires in relation to motherhood, let's bring them before our loving God. Ask Him to pour out His healing and comfort upon your heart. Remember, you don't have to journey alone. Seek out a trusted individual or Christian counseling services that can provide compassionate support and guidance. Your heart deserves healing, and there are resources available to assist you along the way.

CONTRACEPTION[11]

When I first suspected I had endometriosis, I went to the gynecologist and told him my symptoms as well as my suspected diagnosis. He es-

---

[10]Potential causes include hormone disruptors in our personal care products and food, and prolonged use of hormonal birth control. Shanna H. Swan and Stacey Colino, "Reproductive Problems in Both Men and Women Are Rising at an Alarming Rate," *Scientific American*, March 16, 2021, https://www.scientificamerican.com/article/reproductive-problems-in-both-men-and-women-are-rising-at-an-alarming-rate/.

Nayana Talukdar, Yaakov Bentov, Paul T. Chang, Navid Esfandiari, Zohreh Nazemian, and Robert F. Casper, "Effect of Long-Term Combined Oral Contraceptive Pill Use on Endometrial Thickness," *Obstetrics & Gynecology* 120, no. 2 (August 2012): 348–54. Doi:10.1097/AOG.0b013e31825ec2ee.

[11]As a general disclaimer, this section is NOT medical advice. It's simply a reflection of my convictions and opinion.

sentially told me, "It doesn't really matter what you have. We treat all painful periods the same way. Here is some birth control."

I wish I'd spoken up and demanded a better answer from him. But in reality, I was excited at the thought of popping a pill and my problems going away. As a twentysomething young woman, I was also excited at the idea of my skin clearing up and maybe getting some curves on my ruler-shaped body as a result of the hormones from the contraceptive pill.

I returned home with my box of birth control pills and headed to Google to look for positive stories on my specific prescription. Even after intentionally looking for good reviews, all I could find were horror stories. Women bleeding for months on end, increased pelvic pain, digestive issues, and hormonal depressive episodes. Naturally, this scared me.

I spent the next few weeks researching hormonal birth control and how it works in the body. I researched how it interacts with endometriosis, and I was horrified. From all I was reading, I concluded that not only would I find no solution to my endometriosis from these pills, but they might also make it worse (I recommend researching estrogen dominance if you're interested).

When my surgeon agreed with my decision not to use hormonal contraception as a means of treating my endometriosis, citing that it doesn't actually get rid of the disease and simply adds more hormones to the body, I was relieved and curious what other female problems were lazily having synthetic hormones thrown at them. It turns out, most of them.[12]

When I was preparing to get married, I was searching for a way to do family planning without burdening my body with the toxic load of synthetic hormones and chemicals. I also wanted to go about fam-

---

[12]"Birth Control Pills: Medical Uses," Center for Young Women's Health (CYWH), last modified August 11, 2022, https://youngwomenshealth.org/guides/medical-uses-of-the-birth-control-pill/.

ily planning in a way that left room for God to override our timing if we were missing His plan. I believe that God allows us to discern His timing in when we become pregnant, but I also believe that as humans we don't always hear His voice perfectly. If I confuse my timing with God's timing for a baby, I want Him to have room to bring life through me!

Through my involvement in the pro-life movement, I had learned about the potential abortifacient properties of many of the available contraceptives on the market. I also wanted something that honored my body and didn't alter the way God created me. The same goes for my husband. God created our bodies with certain hormones and functions that we wanted to honor in our process of avoiding pregnancy and then conceiving.

In my research, I stumbled across NFP, or natural family planning. There are countless methods that are included in NFP, but the basic principle is body literacy through fertility awareness. I read *Taking Charge of Your Fertility* and started learning how to track my cycle. There was so much more to my cycle than what I had ever learned before!

Learning not just the way menstrual cycles function but the intricacies of my unique cycle was empowering. For the first time in my life, I really understood what was happening in my body at different times of the month.

Unlike the rhythm method of our grandmothers' generation, fertility awareness is something beneficial for all women—not just those who are married (sexually active)! Understanding the different nutritional and energy needs that our bodies have depending on what phase of our cycle we are in, learning how to conceive or avoid conception and recognizing when something is off are just a few of the major benefits of learning the fertility awareness method.

If you are married and trying to prevent pregnancy, the fertility awareness method allows you freedom in how you handle your fertile window.

Fertility awareness is something I will be teaching any future daughters from their first cycle. Our schools are so busy teaching teens how not to get pregnant and spread STDs that they don't teach them the beautiful design of their own bodies. Understanding our cycles and the capacity of our own fertility is one of the ways we can take back our fruitfulness from the feminist cult.

JOURNALING:

- Have you ever considered ways you can honor your body through how you go about family planning? What does it mean to honor your body and its unique design? How can you honor the sanctity of life in how you go about preventing pregnancy?

- Our bodies hold amazing wisdom, including the intricate hormonal cycles that shape our reproductive system. Have you taken the time to learn about your own anatomy and understand the signs of any potential issues? Let go of any shame or discomfort you may have felt in seeking knowledge about your cycle and the remarkable workings of your body.

DEEPER DIVE:

- How can we as Christian women embrace a body-positive and sex-positive perspective while also embracing God's values for sex and sexuality?

SECTION III

Relating to the Men in Our Lives

"I have often recalled that glory is revelation. God glorifies himself when he reveals himself as he is. Jesus Christ glorifies God when he reveals him to us as the God of love who is also the Father. We ourselves are called upon to be the glory of God as we are his image, as we show by what we are who is the God to whom we bear witness. In this passage [1 Corinthians 11:7] Paul then adds that the woman is the glory of man: she reveals him; she shows what a human being truly is.

—JACQUES ELLUL,
The Subversion of Christianity

CHAPTER 7

WE NEED EACH OTHER

"EVERY MAN HAS THE CAPABILITY OF BEING TENDER, ROMANTIC, AND ADORING, IF THESE PASSIONS ARE AWAKENED IN HIM BY THE WOMAN."

—HELEN B. ANDELIN, Fascinating Womanhood

Growing up in my hyperfeminine family did little to help prepare me for marriage to a very masculine man. Like many girls who grew up in a traditional Christian family, I dreamed of the day I would marry my Prince Charming. Even with my feminist leanings, my dreams about my future husband remained mostly untouched by the progressive ideals I embraced in other areas of my life. This is partly because my parents have a healthy and loving traditional marriage—and partly because my desire for marriage had cemented itself in my heart long before my views on men became radicalized. I lived very traditionally, even when embracing less-traditional views, because my belief was that feminism was simply the right for women to choose which path was best for them. The path I wanted was traditional marriage.

When I envisioned my future marriage, I pictured someone like the men I saw in movies. Someone who would innately understand my feelings and emotions, who would want to spend every waking moment with me, who would desire to join me in my fight for women, and who could care less if I didn't take his last name. Now, as a married person, I look back and laugh as I realize that most of my years were spent longing for a male clone of myself.

This desire kept my standards almost impossible to fulfill, as the men who came close to fitting that description tended to have feminine traits that I was not attracted to. The men that I was attracted to didn't fit my description in most other ways. My impossible ideal man, my extremely low self-esteem, and the fact that I was very open with my desire to save any form of sexual relationship with a man until marriage meant that I didn't date much.

My parents had encouraged my sisters and me not to date until we were old enough to start thinking about marriage. They also encouraged us to save the sexual part of our relationships as we got to know the men we were interested in. Unlike many other women who grew up in purity culture, my parents always emphasized that this was not because sex was evil; rather, sex is such a powerful way of connecting that it could add confusion to the process of picking a mate.

In college, I began to question this narrative until I watched my close friends experience profound levels of pain and betrayal because of the sexual relationships they engaged in. They had felt used and discarded by some of the guys in our friend group. The aftermath of those relationships began to overshadow their friendships, their educational pursuits, and destroy their mental health. My heart broke for them, so I decided to learn from their pain and avoid the pitfalls that had in many ways stolen their college years.

At twenty-five, I met my husband, Chris. We both quickly knew we had found our person. This revelation was exciting, but also upped the intensity of our relationship from moment one. Two weeks after we met, I won Miss Tennessee USA, and the next day he asked me to be his girlfriend. We were trying to get to know each other, navigate a long-distance relationship, and figure out how to live a normal life amid my new responsibilities preparing for Miss USA.

On top of these practical challenges, Chris is also ten years older than I am and we came from very different backgrounds. I was projecting a false sense of confidence that I had developed to succeed in the pageant world, but inside I was crippled by insecurity. I hadn't even had my first kiss, and I was suddenly dating a thirty-five-year-old who had made very different choices sexually before finding the Lord. To top it all off, I was clueless about how men thought and interacted in the world. Most of what I knew about men came from movies (which I later found out were written by women), and from what feminism had told me about them. Neither of these sources was much help when it came to interacting with a real man.

Our dating and engagement period were extremely emotional and filled with a lot of challenges. Chris had perspectives and attitudes he needed to address and change, but a lot of what needed to change was me. We had a deep love and respect for one another, and both of us felt a strange sense of peace from the Lord in the midst of navigating some very difficult relational dynamics. Those things kept us together when I think many couples would have called it quits.

We would have a few "good" weeks followed by a few horrible ones, but we kept fighting for our future together. We did some pretty intensive premarital counseling where I learned that I struggle with codependency. I spent months healing the parts of my heart that had been seeking my identity in Chris instead of the Lord. The breakthrough both of us experienced as a result helped us feel ready for marriage.

After getting married, I had hoped the good times would flow more easily, but the opposite happened. Now that he was "stuck" with me, I sunk back into my codependent insecurity. In response to my hyperemotional interactions, Chris shut down emotionally. We were both miserable.

During my time as Miss Tennessee USA, I had become disillusioned with even the word "feminist." After spending my 513-day reign trying to reclaim the word, I gave up. For all the world's so-called women's empowerment, I didn't feel empowered during my reign. I felt that I was only as good as my list of accomplishments. I felt I had to downplay the significance of my relationship with Chris so that I would appear more dedicated to my goals. I felt that no one really cared about me being myself as a role model for young girls—instead, they wanted me to be a billboard for sponsors and "girlboss" culture. While I had wonderful people who supported me personally in Tennessee, people who loved and championed me, the culture felt anything but pro-woman.[1]

What about the women who had chosen motherhood? What about the religious sisters in the Catholic Church who have dedicated their entire lives to serving others? What about the conservative women who have broken ground in their states as the first female governors? What about the wives and mothers of many of the most successful men in the world? Were they not worthy of being considered role models? Why was it that only those of us who were willing to bare all in the bikini competition, work tirelessly to achieve in every area of our lives, and promote the newest feminist ideology on social media were "worthy?" I couldn't unsee it. Feminism wasn't interested in supporting ALL

---

[1] The director of the Tennessee pageant, as well as many of the sponsors I had the privilege of working with, were an exception to much of the toxic pageant world culture that can exist. After competing in other states, the Tennessee program is a breath of fresh air! Kim Greenwood runs her pageant with integrity and honor and truly loves her girls.

women—only the women who bought into the leftist ideology that feminism accompanies.

JOURNALING:

- How have movies, social media, or TV shows impacted your perceptions of men? Do you try to place feminine standards on the men in your life?

- Have you considered yourself a feminist? Do you feel like the unique challenges you face as a woman are talked about by the feminist movement?

MARRIED AND MISERABLE

I found myself three months married and miserable. My feminism hadn't helped prepare me to succeed in marriage—in fact, none of my accomplishments were of any use in my new role. I sat in my reading nook and cried out to God. My disenchantment with feminism, liberalism, and my own marriage dynamics made me desperate for anything the Lord wanted to communicate to me—even if it stung.

I thought God would be most interested in dealing with the many flaws of my husband, but instead, He began to convict me. How fun. He opened my eyes to the ways I had allowed feminism to influence my perspective of what marriage should look like and my reading of the Bible. God was asking me to let go of any agenda I had and simply seek His plan for my marriage. He whispered into my heart, "Chris is the best gift I will ever give you." I clung to that promise as I navigated the disappointments that I was facing in our relationship.

One of the major agendas I brought to my reading of Scripture was my long-held belief that Jesus would have been a feminist if He had come to earth in modern times. This meant that anything Paul said that sounded remotely against my feminist worldview, I came up with an excuse to dismiss. My feminist God would not possibly ask wives to submit to their husbands. He would not say that men are the heads of their families. And He certainly wouldn't promote a male-centric authority structure in the Church.

In reality, I was afraid that researching these verses with any sort of openness would end in the realization that God cares far less about me than he does about men. But my heavenly Father asked that I open myself to any possible application of His Word and trust that the Holy Spirit, not feminism, would guide me into truth. As when God asked Abraham to sacrifice his only son, God was asking me to sacrifice my entire vision of myself as a woman.

As I began to practice what I was reading in the Bible in my own marriage, something beautiful happened. I submitted to Chris as the leader of our family and stopped trying to have everything my way. This created trust in both of us as I let go of control. I started actively looking for ways to honor Chris and the burden that he carried as the leader of our family, instead of allowing insecurity to tell me that I was inferior because I served a different role. This created a beautiful dynamic between him and me.

Chris felt respected, and in turn, his heart toward me became soft, and I felt cherished by him for the first time. I couldn't believe that embracing these old-fashioned and very anti-feminist practices brought more peace and genuine love to our relationship than I could have dreamed of. Far from making me feel subjugated or inferior to men, I saw that when I put my focus on building Chris up as a man, it elicited from him a natural response of celebrating and cherishing me like the Disney princesses I had envied as a little girl. I could suddenly see the intentionality of God. As I laid down my pride and supposed "rights," the very things I had been fighting and demanding to feel from Chris came about naturally.

This transformation motivated me to keep pursuing a deeper understanding of why God's principles in Scripture were producing so much life. I knew there had to be psychological and scientific reasons that His ways worked.

Quickly, I realized I knew nothing about men and how their brains work. Feminism had sold me on the claim that men and women are the same and the only differences that existed were culturally instilled in men. This meant that if a man, such as my husband, did not understand my feelings and emotions, it was not because we are wired differently; rather, it was because he was choosing not to understand me. When I learned about just how different we are—from our brains to our needs in life—I realized how much feminism had damaged my relationship with the men in my life.

I read the book *Fascinating Womanhood* by Helen B. Andelin and was in awe of how well these principles worked not only in my relationship with Chris but also in my relationship with my dad. I started intentionally honoring my dad for the leadership role he played in our family and going to him for marriage advice. I realized that I wasn't going to see growth in my marriage by getting more validation for how I felt. Instead, I sought to understand my husband's male mind more. All of these efforts produced a change in Chris and our marriage dynamic, and I could honestly, finally, say that he was the best gift God had ever given me.

JOURNALING:

- What do you think about the idea of biblical submission to your husband? What does "submission" mean? Are there practical ways you can embrace submission in your life right now?

- It's important to acknowledge instances where the idea of submission has been misused or misunderstood. Have you witnessed such situations? What aspects do you believe were missed or overlooked in these cases? Additionally, have you ever felt resistance toward the concept of submission due to its associations with abuse?

"The idea that love is a holy affair is something intuitively understandable to a woman."

—TEHILLA ABRAMOV, The Secrets of Jewish Femininity

I DREAMED OF MARRIAGE

I dreamed of marriage for most of my life. Fifteen years before I even met my husband, I had our wedding planned on Pinterest. I watched *Say Yes to the Dress* religiously and just knew that I was going to wear a blush pink Alfred Angelo ballgown. (Spoiler alert: I didn't.) If thinking about marriage translated to marriage preparedness, I was beyond prepared.

But despite all the time I had spent daydreaming of marriage, I was not ready when the time came. My mother, grandmother, and aunts had all gotten married in their late teens and early twenties. But here I was, twenty-six years old and still struggling with letting go of my career ambitions in order to unite my life with Chris's. I resented Chris for the fact that I couldn't be the wife he needed and pursue my "dream."

The reality was that my lifelong dream had been to be a wife and mother. I only felt that this dream wasn't good enough because of the pressure I experienced as a successful college student pageant

WE NEED EACH OTHER | 151

titleholder. I felt an insane amount of obligation to constantly achieve more, but it's hard to one-up competing at Miss USA, as you're statistically more likely to play in the Super Bowl than to walk the Miss USA stage.

My years spent undoing my leftist and feminist ideology had re-awakened my passion for politics—"future president" sweater and all. It made sense to me to run for political office in my state and leverage my momentum after I was crowned Miss Tennessee USA. Chris, who is almost always supportive of my crazy pursuits, wasn't convinced it was the right time.

Coming out of an almost two-year season of our lives revolving around my duties as Miss Tennessee, the irony of the resentment I felt toward Chris for not prioritizing me is painfully obvious. He had driven back and forth from where he was living in Ohio to see me in Nashville regularly. He was at every major event I had to attend and used his professional skills as a photographer to help me stay competitive on social media as I was preparing for the national competition—not to mention all his encouragement and frequent pep talks.

My natural selfishness combined with leftover internalized feminism had convinced me that Chris should be willing to do whatever it took to help me realize my next career goal. Forget about the fact that I also expected to start having kids as soon as we were married. I was fixated on making sure Chris was going to love me like Christ loved the church and lay down his life for me. But I thought very little about whether I was following through on my end of that deal.

After processing my disappointment at Chris's lack of enthusiasm for my political aspirations with my mom, I felt a pang of conviction in my chest. The conviction came with loving compassion from my heavenly Father. He could see that much of my ambition was fueled by a profound feeling of personal insignificance. Of course, I love politics and would have enjoyed aspects of running for office, but my real motivation was that same childhood desire to prove myself to the world.

As it often does, insecurity blinded me to my own selfishness. I felt God holding me close as He began to speak to my heart about what I was truly desiring. I was a few months away from my wedding, and He knew that my ultimate desire was to be an amazing wife to my husband and begin cultivating the skills I would need as a mother.

Up to that point, there had never been a time in my life that I didn't have a big ambitious goal that I was working toward. God asked me to let go of my need for a plan and instead embrace the mundane tasks of caring for my new home and husband while working full-time for my parents' ministry. It was challenging when people would ask me, "So what's next?" My answer was, "Being a wife!" My ego hurt a bit, but I knew I needed a paradigm shift to value the very important new role God had given to me.

I never call my wife "wife": I call her "home"—for it is she who makes my home.

—TALMUD, SHABBAT 118B

I KISSED DATING HELLO

If you're hoping to find a husband and start a family, I have good news for you: Marriage is God's call for most people! It is through marriage that the masculine and feminine images of God come together once again to form one flesh. Our very anatomy speaks to this God-ordained purpose for our lives.

Paul says that the love of husbands and wives is a reflection of the mystery of Jesus and His bride, the Church:"'Therefore a man shall leave his father and mother and hold fast to his wife, and the two shall become one flesh.' This mystery is profound, and I am saying that it refers to Christ and the church" (Ephesians 5:31–32).

Growing up in the Church, I frequently saw women in their late twenties, thirties, and forties who desired to be married but still weren't. I could see the pain of disappointment that many of them experienced. The "advice" that I heard repeated to these women, and then to me when I was single a little longer than people expected, seemed to be more damaging than it was helpful.

"As soon as you stop looking, that's when God will bring him!"

"You just have to lay down this idol of marriage in order for God to bring you a husband."

"Maybe you are called to singleness."

I don't know where people came up with this stuff, but as I've processed why it bothered me so much, I realized they definitely didn't get it from the Bible. There is nothing in the Bible that says we have to manipulate God into bringing us a partner. There is nothing in the Bible that says desiring marriage, a picture of Christ and the Church, is idolatry. And it is my perspective that very few people are truly called to singleness.

God wants you to have the companionship and the refining that marriage brings! You'll always be half in and half out, looking for signs that God doesn't support your relationship if you think there's a significant possibility He's chosen you for singleness.

Again, this is just my opinion, but I think God's reasons for calling someone to singleness are typically pretty practical: You're called to serve in a mission field that having a traditional nuclear family would hinder, or your purpose would prevent you from being the kind of wife and mother that God asks us to be, etc. This is clearly the case with Paul's call to singleness. He could not have been a good husband and done all he did to help the formation of the early church if he'd married.

I'll say it again for the ladies in the back: It is good that you desire marriage! It is good that you are motivated to pursue this desire! It is good that you are looking! Unless you have a very clear purpose that requires singleness, marriage has the possibility of bringing the highest level of fulfillment and refinement to the lives of you and your spouse.

Dating and finding a spouse is another area feminism has sought to hijack. Sometimes it's helpful to go back to the basics as we dismantle ways of thinking about men and relationships that are damaging to our process. Fundamentalism has told us that dating and actively seeking marriage is bad. Feminism has told us that committed relationships are a prison and keep us from true liberation.

There's a middle ground of truth that each of us must discern. Marriage is not for the faint of heart, but the struggles it brings help smooth out our rough edges and make us more like Jesus.

A few of my sisters and I attended a Christian ministry school during our college years, and each of us have pretty wild stories of the crazy ways Christians use God to excuse their toxic behavior in dating. For example, a friend of ours had a crush on a guy at school, and when he found out, he let her know he wasn't going to date her because he knew she wasn't his wife. Not because they didn't share values or because he was concerned with her character. Not even because he wasn't attracted to her. How did he know she wasn't his wife? Because he had told God that he expected an actual diamond to appear in his hand when He revealed his future wife to him. I wish this was a joke.

While waiting on a supernatural diamond is a less common story, I would hear other stories of people not even giving someone a chance because they hadn't had a revelation from God that this person was going to be their spouse. While it is obviously important to discern if the Holy Spirit is saying "no" about a potential spouse, I wonder how often people miss out on finding an amazing partner because they have a false belief that some miracle needs to accompany their meeting.

The most common roadblock I see women encounter on their journey to their spouse is an obsession with finding "the one." God will be as involved as we invite Him to be in our dating lives. He can empower us with the wisdom to pick the best kind of man to marry. Sometimes this looks like a sudden supernatural revelation, but what's way more common is eventually landing in the right place with the right person after we've trusted God to guide us each step of the way.

Part of why I don't like the focus on finding "the one" is that I've seen way too many women use it as an excuse to do absolutely nothing. Sitting around at home, making no effort to better themselves, just waiting for God to drop their husband at their doorstep. It's just not gonna happen!

Asking God to lead us to the best career, friendships, and marriage doesn't mean we don't play a part. God promised Abraham land, but Abraham had to get off his butt (as an old man) and go take it. James 2:20 says faith (believing that God can and will do something) without works (us taking action) is dead. Ninety-nine percent of the time, supernatural stories require natural cooperation from us.

The fact that God can reveal our spouse to us supernaturally, through a dream, vision, or revelation, should not put pressure on us if He doesn't do it that way. Your marriage won't be any better because you had a dream about your husband before you met him. If the stars align to spell out the name of the man you marry, or you realize you want to marry him over the course of getting to know him in a very mundane way, you will still have the same highs and lows. Faith and trust will still be required of you.

Don't put pressure on yourself to have a crazy revelatory experience in order to know you're with someone who is good for you and who will be a godly husband. God gave you a brilliant mind that can also make spiritually sound decisions without having to see the heavens open over the head of the man you are considering.

That said, when my dad realized my mom was "the one," it was very supernatural. God literally said, "That's her!" before my dad even knew my mom well. This can absolutely happen, but it is the exception rather than the rule! My dad also didn't use this revelation to try to manipulate my mom. He was still willing to pursue and date her, winning her heart over without making her feel the pressure of "God said!" For the love of God, please do not tell someone whom you are still getting to know, "God told me we're going to get married." You will either weird the other person out or make them feel pressured to "obey" God. Just wait and test what God has communicated. It'll happen if it's His will, and if not, you'll be glad you didn't share an incorrect revelation.

The final reason I don't think it's helpful to obsess over "the one" is that when we get it wrong, there are major consequences. I have seen girls marry horrible men because they convinced themselves God was telling them to. I've also seen couples who have been together for a number of weeks have zero emotional or physical boundaries because they already "knew" they would be getting married. Often, they did not get married and had a huge mess of emotional and physical ties to undo.

I'm going to go out on a limb here and say that God will never tell you to marry someone abusive, someone who refuses to marry you, someone who is not a believer, or someone who you have no respect for or attraction to. God's plan for marriage does not include being abused or manipulated, and it also doesn't require you to be with someone who repulses you. Physical attraction isn't the most important determining factor in who you'll marry, but it's definitely part of the equation!

I came of age around the height of the purity culture movement. Books like *I Kissed Dating Goodbye* and *When God Writes Your Love Story* had a cult-like following. In response to the rising popularity of hookup culture and casual dating, young Christians were seeking better ways to handle their love lives. It's my perspective that many of these new ideas were the result of the pendulum swinging too far the other way. Finding casual sex (understandably) unattractive, many young believers resorted to the opposite extreme: simply shutting down their love lives altogether until God deposited the right person at their doorstep.

Unlike the title of Josh Harris's infamous *I Kissed Dating Goodbye*, most of us need to kiss dating hello. Intentional dating, which involves consulting our mentors and close friends, can be a huge help in finding a partner in life. Few of us have really seen healthy dating, but it is possible.

This doesn't have to look like the sometimes high-pressure blind date scene. Intentional dating can be as simple as letting the trustworthy people in your life know that you would like to be married and are open to meeting their single friends. For most women, we know who the "no's" are right away, and then there is another category of "maybe's" that we shouldn't be afraid to intentionally get to know.

I have friends who won't go out on one-on-one dates, but even this conviction doesn't have to be a hindrance to dating intentionally. Getting to know men around friends and family is a totally viable way to find someone, and you'll probably be able to easily weed out men who don't share your values by doing things this way.

Personally, I went on a fair number of dates to get to know guys I was interested in, but I had clear boundaries that I maintained about things like how late we were out, how late I texted with them, physical proximity, etc. As a married woman, I can say I genuinely don't have any dating regrets because I stuck with my boundaries.

Even though it's important to get out there and meet potential matches, there are definitely seasons when we should not be dating. I don't want to be too specific here because I think this varies by individual, but generally speaking, if you aren't ready to get married, it's not a great time to date.

Maybe you disagree with me on this, and that's okay! There are always exceptions to these things that aren't black and white in Scripture. Maybe you met your husband and started dating in high school, or perhaps you feel high school is a good time to "practice" dating.

I hold the more traditional view that while God can absolutely connect you to the right person before you're ready for marriage, you're going to make things more complicated for yourself if you pursue the relationship anyway. Especially if you're saving sexual intimacy for marriage, the temptation can become more intense the longer you put off getting married.

While you could meet Mr. Right at any time, looking for him when you're going through a really difficult time in your relationship with God, are in the throes of addiction, or during an extremely emotionally unhealthy period are all examples of times when it would probably be better to put your energy into yourself rather than into dating. Ideally, we are always working to become healthier and stronger versions of ourselves, but in crisis seasons, it's important to really focus on your own healing and reconciliation with Father God. Don't be so obsessed with "perfecting" yourself that you never step out and meet amazing men, but also don't neglect seasons of refining.

I would have saved myself a whole lot of heartache by searching for a good man instead of Prince Charming. Prince Charming is the ideal man that many of us compare all other men to. Unfortunately, he is not real, and our vision of him has been primarily formed by the media we consume and our natural desire to be with someone similar to us.

A good man, on the other hand, has specific character traits and common values with us, but everything else is up for discussion. His eye color, style, and interests play almost no role in who he is as a man. He is like a car with a reliable engine, safe frame, and good tires. The color, sound system, and other bells and whistles are just an added bonus, but they shouldn't be the most important part of your search for a car.

The Prince Charming ideal has the potential to blind you to countless good men in your life and can also cause you to be overly critical of your husband once you have him. I found that I held Chris to standards that were straight out of a Disney movie. These standards weren't based on biblical ideals; rather, they were based on my desire to feel like a princess.

When I let go of this imaginary dream man and instead embraced my husband for the many strengths he brought to the table, our relationship improved greatly. If you are serious about getting married, you are going to have to drop some of the unnecessary ideals you have internalized. Too often I hear women describing this as "settling." But real settling is marrying a man who lacks strength of character and shared values with you (more on this in a minute). It is not settling to let go of specific expectations about a man's appearance, the kind of car he drives, his taste in movies and music, or other similarly unimportant issues.

I have watched so many sharp women of God accidentally choose singleness for themselves by majoring on the minors. I have also watched other beautiful women subject themselves to horrible men whose character was completely lacking simply because they had a few interests and passions in common.

In the 2009 film *He's Just Not That Into You*, twentysomething-year-old Gigi is stuck in a pattern that many of us and our friends have found ourselves in before. Giving way too much time and attention to men who just aren't that into her, Gigi finds herself heartbroken in her search for love. After every date, she would wait for the guy to call her and ask her out again, but time and time again, he didn't. Her friends try to help boost her confidence, but they never point out the obvious: These guys are just not into her.

If a man is a potential partner for you, he will make himself available to you. Don't overlook obvious signs that a guy is just not interested. If he isn't clearly pursuing you, you can safely mark him off your mental list of potential suitors. Obviously, some give-and-take during the getting-to-know-you stage is necessary. Men want to know if you are interested in getting to know them too! But if you are primarily pursuing him without much reciprocation, it's time to move on.

The most painful examples of what I will call "Gigi syndrome" are when I have seen intelligent, godly women get stuck obsessing over a guy who has made it clear he is never going to pursue her. Do not convince yourself that this will change. Most likely, you don't even like who this man really is and are just obsessing over the idea of him that you have created in your mind. Even if you think you know him well, after being married, I can tell you that you don't really know someone until you've been through trial and difficulty together.

If you think you might have Gigi syndrome, please do yourself a huge favor and let that man go. If you find yourself stuck, seek the Lord and maybe even a counselor to help you figure out why. Sometimes we can trick ourselves into thinking that the solution to our insecurities is pining after an impossible man.

I have compiled a list of what I consider to be some of the most important red flags and green flags in a potential mate. When you read through them, ask yourself if any apply to you as well! None of us is perfect, but it's great to always work toward becoming better versions of ourselves—especially if we are seeking to attract an amazing man of God.

RED FLAGS IN A POTENTIAL MATE:

- Pride
- Active addiction to porn, drugs, alcohol, phone, video games, TV, etc.
- Treats his parents badly
- Self-absorbed: He doesn't listen, he interrupts, he's inconsiderate
- Lack of ambition
- Lack of discipline
- He pushes you to be overly emotionally or physically intimate
- He doesn't value health
- He is stagnant
- He is controlling or manipulative
- He is abusive in any way
- He isn't making the effort to pursue you
- He doesn't share your values
- He makes you feel bad for needing alone time or time with friends
- He isn't a believer
- His faith isn't strong

GREEN FLAGS IN A POTENTIAL MATE:

- He is a man of character; he is attentive, dependable, honest, consistent, generous, humble, and kind

- He has a strong relationship with God
- He encourages you in your walk with God without condemning you
- He is a hard worker
- He has a pattern of growing and learns from his mistakes
- He is open about any struggles he has or has had in the past with addictions
- You share your major values; this includes what size family you want, what type of faith community you want to be involved in, if you want to homeschool your kids or put them in public school, how you handle finances, your perspectives on gender roles, etc.
- He pursues a relationship with you
- He has mentors who he seeks wisdom from

JOURNALING:

- Have you considered the beautiful truth that, most likely, God desires you to be married? Take a moment to reflect on this notion. Do you believe in His good plans for you? If not, what do you think is hindering your faith in His intentions? Have you ever been made to feel that desiring marriage is idolatrous? If you are already married, let your pen become a vessel of prayer, seeking the Holy Spirit's guidance to see His intentional hand at work in your marriage, especially during challenging seasons.
- What do you think about the idea that marriage is like a combo of the masculine and feminine qualities of God? How do you see our culture downplaying the significance of having both masculine and feminine aspects in a marriage?

- Have you ever gotten any advice about dating from fellow believers that was just plain bad or didn't help at all? How can you switch up the way you talk about this stuff to be more supportive and uplifting for your single friends who are waiting for their perfect match?

- Explore the ways you can make yourself more available to potential mates. Are there ways in which you have concealed yourself instead of venturing out and engaging with men? What whispers of guidance do you feel God imparting in this area of your life?

- Think about how discernment has played a role in your dating experiences. How do you strike a balance between seeking divine guidance and relying on the common sense God has given you?

- How have you set and respected boundaries in your dating life? Reflect on any moments where you wish you had done things differently or instances where you successfully maintained boundaries. How do boundaries contribute to healthier relationships and self-respect?

"There's a Jewish idea that men have more laws pertaining to them because it is hard for them to understand their identity without the "doing" whereas women naturally understand it is WHO they are."

—RABBI SHAIS TAUB

EAGLES AND COMPLIMENTS?

The undoing of my feminist theology was shocking. It was shocking to me, most of all, but also shocking to my friends and family, who couldn't believe I was crediting Paul with giving me transformative marriage advice. I kept it mostly to myself in the beginning, but eventually, people were asking what had made such a difference in our relationship.

Expecting that my perspective would be met with the feminist skepticism I had lived in for years, I would cautiously begin to lay out the many parts of my paradigm shift. To my surprise, other women were largely receptive to the information I was sharing. It was like I had discovered an ancient secret to improving male-female relationships, and the women I spoke to, burned on the feminist advice they'd been receiving, were hungry for a different viewpoint. There was something in the words of Paul that appealed to a self-evident truth that many of us had experienced in our relationships.

As much as it initially hurt our pride, many of us were waking up to the peace that this truth was bringing to our relationships—a peace that feminism, with its cries for constant revolution, didn't even pretend to offer.

For years I had been unwilling to even consider that God would place any gender-specific expectations on His people. It was too old-fashioned and definitely too sexist, and I knew God was not sexist toward His creation. I took these expectations into my reading of Scripture, and rather than allowing God's Word to speak for itself and challenge me, I manipulated the text to say what I wanted it to say. I convinced myself that the Bible was some sort of feminist literature hidden behind bad translations. I found teachings to back up what I wanted the Bible to say and shared these views with others as often as possible.

I didn't read Scripture this way because I was stupid or had some sort of evil agenda. I did it because I was scared. My experiences with men and the world around me kept me from using my mind and instead required me to use my emotions in interpreting God's plan for male and female gender roles.

Growing up in a very conservative homeschool community meant that I interacted with a lot of real sexism. As I mentioned before, many of my friends' fathers and brothers not only believed that God had different roles for men and women, but also that their value to God was different. My perception was that the women in these families were treated by their husbands and fathers as second-class citizens in their own homes—and worse yet, they told the women in their lives that God also saw them this way.

The terms "egalitarianism" and "complementarian" might or might not be new to you. They are umbrella terms that are used in theology to refer to two of the most common biblical perspectives on gender roles. While theological ideas aren't always very exciting to talk about, it's very important that we understand these terms for the sake of how we live our lives. Our perspective on gender roles affects every relationship in our lives—from how we interact with our fathers, to whom we date, to how we serve in our church communities. Having a consistent principle for reading and applying Scripture that talks about gender roles helps us have more "guideposts" in our search for truth.

Christianity as a distinct religion from Judaism was formed mainly in Rome and Greece. This means there were many Greek and Roman influences in the formation of our faith history. Christianity seems to have adopted the Greek view of women as either a whorish distraction from that which is truly holy or as little more than an animal in value—only useful for sexual fulfillment.

This is very likely because those who translated Paul's letters from Greek to other languages used other Greek documents from his time period as a reference. Inevitably, the humanistic perspective of men and women and their sexuality found its way into the translated text, but it was influenced by how people living in Greece and Rome at the time interpreted and applied Paul's letters.[2]

Egalitarianism is the perspective that there are no gender roles, and instead, Scripture promotes complete equality between men and women. This equality is not just in our value but also in our roles. It is right in line with the feminist perspective that the only differences between men and women are those that are socialized into us. Egalitarians view baby boys and girls as the same blank canvases that society "forces" masculine and feminine characteristics onto.

In response to the broken perspective of women that was accepted in ancient Greece, modern progressive Christianity has rejected the writings of Paul altogether as being toxically patriarchal and backward. Embracing an overly egalitarian view of women, they have accepted a reduction of their feminine design in exchange for "equality." There can be no appreciation of the unique gifts and perspectives that women have to offer because any acknowledgment of differences between men and women is a potential open door for inequality.

COMPLEMENTARIANISM

In contrast to the egalitarian worldview, the complementarian view sees men and women as opposites that complete each other. The root word "complement" points to the complementary roles that men and women play in each other's lives. Our value and worth to God are equal, but our roles and purposes are different. Think yin and yang, two halves of a whole, differently shaped pieces of the same puzzle. If you play an instrument, you understand that part of the beauty of music is the melody and harmony of a song working together to create a beautiful work of art. This is what complementarianism seeks to recognize.

---

[2]John T. Bristow, *What Paul Really Said About Women: The Apostle's Liberating Views on Equality in Marriage, Leadership, and Love* (San Francisco: HarperOne, 1991), 6.

It doesn't seek to subjugate women to an eternal role as second-class citizens, nor does it reduce the image-bearing call on men and women to mere anatomy—although some have tried to do this in the name of complementarianism. True biblical complementarianism sees the incredible opportunity that men and women individually have to represent the masculine and feminine natures of God and will not cheapen itself by claiming this duty is unimportant enough to be obsolete.

The Jewish understanding of women has long been that while our role is different compared to the role of our male counterparts, it is no less important. In fact, many Jews would argue that women and the tasks we have been given by God are even more spiritual in nature than those given to men. The Jewish perspective is especially important because Jesus was raised in Judaism.

Our job as mothers—to grow tiny humans, feed them at our breasts, and provide life-long nurturance to their hearts—is the real stuff of life. Women in Judaism have an immensely smaller burden on them as it relates to following religious law because it is believed that men need more help connecting with God, whereas women have an innate understanding of belonging to Him.[3]

I believe it is safe to say that complementarianism as presented in this book captures ancient truths about men and women, honors the image of God within both sexes, and promotes each of us to a role of immeasurable value, both now and in eternity. This view fits perfectly with the Hebraic perspective of women, and therefore goes hand in hand with what Paul, a Jewish scholar, was REALLY trying to communicate in the epistles.

Yes, he gives boundaries and order to how men and women are to function in the home and the Body of Christ, but he never makes value claims about women being less than men. In fact, he explains that in

---

[3]Manis Friedman, "What Men Don't Understand About Women and Vice Versa," Jewish Learning Institute, video, January 14, 2021, 3:12. https://www.youtube.com/watch?v=5mGAuPcT058.

the Body, men and women are to submit to one another, and in marriage is the only time women are specifically asked to submit to a man. This submission is also not a position of lower importance; rather, it is a means of relinquishing control over our husbands.

Our natural proclivity as women is to nurture and mother those in our circles. However, in our relationship with our husband, we are intended to manifest not as a mother but as the object of their affection and romantic passion. If we do not intentionally hold back our mothering when we interact with our husband, we will not elicit romantic passion from him. Instead, we will become a second mother to him. This has the potential to ruin an otherwise happy marriage.

If you are not married, you might wonder how any of this applies to you. But trust me when I tell you that dismantling any internalized feminism now will have a substantial positive impact on your relationships with other men in your life, as well as your potential future marriage. Each of us have had good and bad interactions with men, and some have even had exceptionally traumatic experiences with men. All of these experiences play into our perspectives of how we believe men and women should function in this world—clouding our ability to look at things without judgment or bias. Our experiences greatly influence the ways we interact with our fathers, brothers, boyfriends, husbands, and even our sons.

I wish someone had told me these truths when I was in high school. I wish I had spent less time daydreaming about how my future husband was going to spoil me and make all my dreams come true and more time learning about how men receive love and respect. While some of the men I was interested in treated me poorly because of their personal shortcomings, some of them treated me poorly because I treated them like women—I wanted them to have an innate understanding of my emotional world, to be as nurturing as my mother, and to enjoy the same movies that I do.

I wish my friends would have had the wisdom to stop telling me I deserved better and to start telling me how to deserve the kind of man I was hoping for. And I wish I had done the same with my friends. Instead of watching them self-destruct after interactions with horrible men, I wish I had looked at them honestly and said, "You are doing this to yourself by giving your attention to toxic men." Like Gigi's revelation in *He's Just Not That Into You,* we can love our friends in a much more authentic way by encouraging them to confront their own toxicity rather than victimizing themselves in every drama.

JOURNALING:

- What do you think about egalitarianism and complementarianism? They're two different ways of looking at gender roles. How do they compare to what you already believe or feel about gender roles?

- Reflect upon the term "complementarianism" and its emphasis on the idea of men and women completing or complementing one another. What does this idea signify to you, dear sister? Do you find yourself in agreement or disagreement with this perspective? Take a moment to discern the reasons behind your stance. Allow your heart and mind to engage in a dialogue, seeking clarity and understanding.

DEEPER DIVE:

- Take some time to research the differences between complementarianism, egalitarianism, soft and hard complementarianism, etc. Which perspective do you think is the most biblically based? Why do you think God would care about defining different roles for men and women? Why do you think this issue has divided Christian groups for so long?

THE EVIL FEMINIST ON YOUR SHOULDER

Whether you're aware of it or not, having grown up as a woman in the Western world, you probably have a feminist sitting on your shoulder. We will call her Karen, for obvious reasons. Picture the old cartoons where an angel and a demon appear on the shoulders of a character who is trying to make a decision about something.

Just like the little demon, she sits there and "helps" remind you that you are oppressed, simply due to your chromosomes. If someone makes a joke about anything remotely feminine, she will let you know. Like a pair of glasses with the wrong prescription, she will change the way that you see the world, but not for the better.

Didn't get a good grade on your final paper? Your professor probably scored you lower because he doesn't like strong women, and not because you struggled with your citations. Got asked to serve in children's ministry at church again instead of being asked to teach the church culture class? Your church probably believes women are second-class citizens who should be relegated to behind-the-scenes work only. Not because women can be trusted more easily with the incredibly important task of discipling the next generation.

Karen is not interested in helping you observe reality and consider all possible reasons for the challenges you are experiencing. She is interested in turning you into a soldier for her feminist army, and she hopes you will recruit others. By convincing you that you are a victim, she motivates you to interact with the men in your life with suspicion rather than trust.

We are constantly looking critically at the movies that are made, the jokes our friends tell, and the way random men in public interact with us. See if this is something you are doing out of habit throughout your week. You are likely interpreting your interactions with men through a critical lens that views their gender as evil.

Even after I had rejected the feminist worldview, it still tainted my ability to approach men with compassion and trust, causing me to be offended by my husband and perpetuating an overall negative perspective of all men.

Karen doesn't limit herself to political issues. Her critical voice greatly affects every facet of our lives—from how we read Scripture to how we interact with our dads, brothers, husbands, and friends. It is not surprising that our broken culture is creating more broken people, but sometimes we are so used to Karen's voice that we confuse it with our own.

So much of what used to offend me in my interactions with men was not rooted in things that were actually offensive; rather, they were things that I was told I should be offended by. My husband pointing out that I tended to be more sensitive in the days leading up to my period, for instance, was a fair observation to make (and honestly helpful for both of us), but I felt I should be offended by it for whatever reason.

You might be shocked to learn how much of our culture has been shaped and influenced by radical feminism because we have accepted so much of it as our own thoughts or as the status quo. Karen was carefully crafted by the founders of the radical feminist movement. They hid her in our movies, our education system, and the speeches of our political leaders. Without even looking for her, she found you and made a comfortable spot for herself, whispering into your ear.

She doesn't care about you having a happy marriage, being a good mom, being fruitful, or finding contentment in the normalcy of life. Instead, she has one goal: to convince you that you are oppressed so that you will help start a revolution and destroy all the systems that evil men have created.

As we discussed in Chapter 2, one of the major pursuits of the radical feminist movement has been to destroy the nuclear family, because feminism sees the interdependence of men and women as a major obstacle to women finding true "equality." The nuclear family relies on certain gender roles being established in order to flourish—women are biologically the only ones capable of birthing and feeding new life, which then requires men to provide both physical protection and financial security for the woman and child that they are responsible for. Much has been done to try and erode this very natural order that happens when humans are left to follow their biological instincts rather than cultural norms. Karen has made huge efforts to tell men and women that this arrangement is sexist, and that men have been brainwashed to protect the women in their lives and expect women to pour their energy into nurturing their children.

Meanwhile, women have been convinced by Karen that it is better to outsource their childbearing, breastfeeding, childcare, and education of their children so that they will have the time and energy to become the "equal" of their male counterparts—climbing the corporate ladder and becoming a formidable careerwoman. We have subconsciously allowed her to tell us that our natural ability to create and nurture new generations of the human race is less valuable than us taking our place as another cog in the machine. The irony is that most women (and men, for that matter) will never have a true career, but will instead simply have a job[4]

And that's the next big thing Karen has tried to brainwash us into believing—that a career could possibly be more rewarding and fulfilling than the lifelong love of a husband and the creation of our own family. It isn't wrong that many women want to have careers outside of caregiving, but we've believed a lie if we think a career is worth sacrificing the deeper things of life for.

---

[4] Jordan Peterson, "Jordan Peterson On 'Most People Don't Have Careers. . .'" Strong Mind Motivation, video, November 11, 2022, 0:29. https://www.youtube.com/watch?v=9nGfcTQLmWs.

As someone who has faced serious health challenges in life and who has also lost many loved ones, it is clear to me that what will matter the most when I am on my deathbed is not what I have accomplished. I will want to know that I loved well, that I served and honored my husband and made his life more significant. I will want to know that I resisted anything that tried to come between me and my family. I will want to know that I fought to protect the important people in my life and that my future generations will be committed to doing the same because of their love for God rather than mere obligation.

JOURNALING:

- In what ways do you think Karen, the feminist on your shoulder, is influencing your perspective? Are there beliefs or opinions that you have adopted without questioning their origin?

- Imagine on your other shoulder that there is an angel who whispers God's truth to you about your identity as a woman. What is she saying to you vs. what Karen is saying?

KILLING KAREN

Killing the feminist on your shoulder (or at least evicting her if death sounds a little too harsh) is a huge first important step in attracting a masculine man. The love of a masculine man enables you to fully surrender to God's feminine design for you. And the reason he will be looking for a feminine woman is so that he can fully surrender to God's masculine design for him.

Karen the Feminist will do her best to prevent you from integrating your life with a good man, surrendering to God's plan for your womanhood, and leaning into the feminine image of God that you are called to share with the world. As long as your loyalty lies with her and her narrative of the world, you will have an extremely difficult time getting along with most men.

What Karen won't tell you about is the incredible fulfillment that comes from a happy marriage. It is genuinely one of the greatest joys in my life to uplift my husband. I find so much purpose in caring for him, body, mind, and spirit. This daily mission to improve his life rather than make it miserable requires that I lean into the Lord's strength.

The beauty is that as I grow in forgiveness, patience, intentionality, and love, I am becoming more like Jesus. This type of transformation wouldn't be possible without the motivation I get from wanting to love my husband well.

JOURNALING

Let's talk about the idea of attracting a masculine man. How could being with a strong and masculine man help you embrace and embody the feminine qualities that reflect God's image?

_____

_____

_____

_____

_____

_____

_____

_____

_____

_____

_____

_____

Dive into the transformative power of forgiveness, patience, intentionality, and love within the context of marriage and relationships. How could your commitment to loving your partner well contribute to your personal growth and help you become more like Jesus?

_____

_____

_____

_____

_____

_____

_____

_____

_____

_____

_____

_____

_____

CHAPTER 8

PURITY CULTURE

"PUT SIMPLY, SEX IS NOT CONSIDERED 'DIRTY,' ONLY REGULATED TO CERTAIN TIMES, CERTAIN PLACES, AND WITH CERTAIN PEOPLE. WITH THOSE PARAMETERS MAINTAINED, SEX IS A HOLY ACT"

—RABBI ELYSE GOLDSTEIN, ReVisions

In high school I had a friend who survived a violent sexual assault. The aftermath profoundly affected her in almost every way, and the trauma negatively redirected the trajectory of her life. Sexual abuse of any kind often derails the lives of its victims.

In college, many of the girls would sneak out of the dorm to hook up with different guys behind the bleachers, in the prayer garden, or anywhere else they could hide. When my friend Melissa and I found time to catch up and get a frozen yogurt together, she told me about her most recent beau. As she described her sneaking around, Melissa shared how empty she felt after these interactions. She told me she felt used even though she freely chose to participate in these hookups.

One day I told Melissa I had a crush on our mutual friend. I went on and on about how cute he was and how much I liked his personality. The next day I ran into her after biology class. "You'll never guess what happened last night!" And she proceeded to tell me that the friend I had a crush on was her most recent hookup.

I was hurt, of course. I had *just* told her that he was someone I was interested in, and now she was spending her time canoodling with him? When I shared my frustration, she stopped me and looked me in the eyes. "Justice, he doesn't deserve you." And she was right. He was looking for cheap thrills.

What is sad is that Melissa thought he *did* deserve her. And even though she didn't directly say it, it was clear that she felt her promiscuity made her less worthy of a quality man.

The obvious impact that sexual interactions and violations have on young women are very clear, so why do we continue to tell women that their sexual choices are "no big deal"? If someone steals your favorite sweater, you don't call it clothing assault. So why does our culture pretend that changing sexual partners is as unimportant as changing sweaters? To be clear, I am not trying to compare sexual assault with the decision to have sex with different partners; rather, I'm simply trying to highlight the hypocrisy of saying sex is significant sometimes but not other times.

It's not clear to me what feminists thought they would accomplish by "sexually liberating" women. Maybe some were eager to undo the shame associated with their own sexual choices. Perhaps others wanted to justify the use of sex as a bargaining tool in male-dominated workplaces. Regardless of their motivation, the mission of "sexual liberation" for women was successful. Unfortunately, the real impact of sexual liberation was sexual enslavement.

Ironically there are only two groups that benefit from women being "sexually liberated": the many men who they sleep with, and the contraception and abortion industries that keep them childless in the process.

I believe the cult-like following of the purity culture movement in the early 2000s was caused by an overreaction to the feminist cries for sexual liberation in the previous generations. My friends' moms, who had experienced the brokenness that resulted from their own sexual liberation, emphatically embraced the message of the purity movement. Far from being motivated by a desire to control women's bodies, I think the majority of people supporting the purity culture movement simply didn't have any other alternatives to the feminist messaging of free love.

If you grew up in the church, you've probably had to undo a lot of the dysfunctional ways of thinking that came along with purity culture—I know I did. But most likely, those perspectives were less damaging than having sex with multiple partners in high school and college would have been. Maybe you've convinced yourself that the sexual relationships of your youth wouldn't have caused you any shame at all if you had not been influenced by the purity movement. Regardless, every sexual interaction has an impact on us. It's important to address any shame that exists in your design as a sexual being because your sexuality is a gift to you from God. Rather than feeling resentment toward the purity movement, try considering the other issues you could be having to resolve if you had gravitated toward sexual liberation.

Telling young women that sex is meaningless is by far the most damaging message we can give them about their sexuality. It invalidates the pain of rejection after a sexual partner is no longer interested in us and the violence of sexual abuse. Without even opening the Bible, we can clearly see that sex has a huge impact on every part of our lives—bodies, minds, and spirits. Sex has the ability to bind us to another human in a deep and meaningful way. When we are constantly giving it away (not just through sexual intercourse but also through other sexual expressions) we dilute its potent powers of connection.

Regardless of your sexual history, it is never too late to reclaim your sexual freedom. Sexual freedom differs from sexual liberation in that it entails using your sexuality to serve your soul and spirit rather than to serve random men who have not earned the reward of your intimacy. Reclaiming your sexuality is a powerful decision to only give the most intimate parts of yourself to a person who is deserving. As a Christian woman, this means the one person who has promised before God to protect, serve, and love you—to lay down their very life for you. That is the only man who is deserving of the parts of you that have the potential to make or break the rest of your life—the parts of you that have the potential to create a new human being who will need your nurturing and support.

JOURNALING:

- Let's talk about society's double standards when it comes to women's sexual choices. Why do you think there's so much emphasis on downplaying the significance of changing sexual partners? Specifically, why do you think this message is often directed toward women, reassuring them that their sexual choices are "no big deal?" What are the potential consequences of this narrative?

- Let's dive into the idea of sexual freedom, as I described it, and how it differs from sexual liberation. What do you think about the concept of reclaiming your sexuality and using it to serve your soul and spirit instead of just engaging with random partners? Do you see this approach as a way to experience true sexual freedom?

MODEST PROBABLY ISN'T HOTTEST

I've found that Christian women are even less open to conversations about modesty than they are about sexual purity. In many ways, I understand why. The way we dress and behave is a massive part of how we express ourselves to the world around us. Acknowledging that there might be any sort of universal guiding principles requires deep trust and humility.

If this discussion is hard for you, I totally get it. I promise to be gracious and leave room for the Holy Spirit to speak to you individually about what modesty will look like for you.

Let's start by talking about what modesty isn't, because these are some of the most common points of concern.

Modesty isn't:

- Taking responsibility for the wrongful actions of others

- Having shame about our bodies

- Only for "holy" people

- Sexist, as there are modesty standards placed on both men and women, although unique to their genders

- One size fits all

- A limitation on creativity in fashion or a passion for the fashion industry

- Anyone else's responsibility to call you out on

- An excuse to shun those who don't attain your level of modesty

- Covering your body to make sure men don't get aroused or telling women they're responsible for men's desires/actions.

Modesty is, however, something that everyone—both women and men—is called to navigate and live out as godly individuals. While the clothing aspect of modesty is often highlighted, modesty also includes the way that we behave. Our behavior needs to reflect modesty—honor of God, honor of our bodies, reverence, regard for others, respect, humility, etc.

Women and men are both called to honor their bodies through modesty in a way that is specific to their gender. In our case, God calls us to dress like women and not like men. Deuteronomy 22:5 says, "A woman shall not wear a man's clothing, nor shall a man put on a woman's clothing; for whoever does these things is an abomination to the Lord your God." Some women may feel convicted to wear only dresses and skirts in order to be both covered and feminine in their appearance. I totally respect this conviction, but my husband and I agree that wearing pants as a woman doesn't have to be masculine.

There aren't any verses that clearly tell us that any parts of our bodies should be covered outside of what is considered nakedness. How covered we need to be is going to be influenced by our cultural standards and the setting we are in. For instance, a swimsuit is probably not the best attire for dinner at a nice restaurant, and a dress that draws a lot of attention to ourselves isn't a great choice for someone else's wedding. The setting matters.

A huge part of modesty for me is considering how others will feel when they are around me. Feminism tells us that we shouldn't have to take responsibility for how others perceive what we wear (especially if we are talking about avoiding arousing men with our clothes). And while I agree that each person is individually responsible for how they react to the clothing choices of others, we are also encouraged in the Bible to be considerate of others in all that we do. This includes what we put on our bodies and how we treat others. Other people don't get to hold us accountable for our choices without our invitation, but God certainly has the right to.

My definition of modesty is submitting to God through all of my actions—the clothes I wear and my behavior. In a practical sense, I am not 100 percent sure what this looks like. I try to dress to make those around me feel comfortable—not holding myself back from self-expression, but not making my self-expression offensive to anyone. For instance, I try to cover up more when I am around my more modest friends and their families. I try to pick clothing that is appropriate to the setting I will be in. I also analyze my intentions when I am dressing, asking myself, "Why am I wearing this and are my motives pure?" I consider dressing in a way that's mindful of others to be an expression of love.

I want other women to feel respected by my clothing and behavior choices. Likewise, when my friends, brothers, husband, and dad are around me, I want to make all of them feel comfortable, too, to the extent that I am able. As someone who has struggled with my fair share of insecurities, I want to do my best to prevent others from feeling insecure. But this in no way means I can't be beautiful. It's important to avoid developing shame or embarrassment about our bodies in our pursuit of modesty. This involves recognizing that not all attention drawn to the body is sexual. As women, we were created to carry God's beauty. Inevitably, that will draw attention to us, and that's okay.

I feel that many Christians have overemphasized modesty and used shame as a tool of manipulation. I wish modesty was modeled more than it is talked about and would love to see women affirming other women in their inner and outer beauty, regardless of whether they fit their personal standards of modesty. I would also like to see the behavioral aspects of modesty emphasized just as much as the clothing side.

There is often an automatic assumption that women who choose to wear dresses, cover their heads, and not show cleavage, etc., are legalistic, but ironically, I have heard more judgment directed toward women who choose to be more covered than from them. Remember that legalism, like modesty, is a heart posture and not a specific set of actions. Tearing other women down publicly or behind their backs because they feel convicted to live differently than you do is just as toxic as the feminism we are trying to dismantle.

JOURNALING:

• Journal about the challenges of discussing modesty within your Christian circles. How do trust and humility play a role in navigating this topic? Acknowledge the difficulty of the conversation and reflect on how you can embrace a gracious and individualized approach.

• Explore the tension between individual responsibility and considering others' perceptions. Reflect on how being considerate of others is an expression of love. How does this align with biblical teachings?

• Dive into the issue of judgment and assumptions within Christian communities about modesty choices. Have you ever called another woman legalistic for embracing a different modesty standard than you? Or perhaps you've judged the hearts of other women who don't dress as modestly as yourself. Reflect on how modesty and legalism are matters of the heart, not just specific actions.

DEEPER DIVE:

• Get your Bible ready! Explore the biblical perspective on gender-specific dress, specifically Deuteronomy 22:5. How can you strike a balance between embracing femininity in your clothing choices and respecting your personal convictions?

ABORTION

The topic of abortion has been present in my life since before I even knew how babies were made. I remember people around me talking about abortion as casually as they talked about what they had for lunch. It was the era of Misty Edwards, The Call, Bound4LIFE, and the International House of Prayer. If you grew up in church at that time, you know exactly the sort of intensity that surrounded the abortion conversation and how important it was in our culture to get kids brought into the message early on.

For those of you who didn't experience this very specific non-denominational charismatic subculture, here is a prayer that my friends and I had memorized in middle school:

Jesus, I plead your blood over my sins and the sins of my nation. God, end abortion and send revival to America.

Revival and abortion weren't just hot topics; they were *the* topics of our generation. When I was around fourteen, I remember buying various colored T-shirts at the thrift store and using a bleach pen to write that prayer on the shirts for my friends and myself.

The Christian media I was consuming, my friends, and my youth leaders were always talking about how evil abortion was—sometimes even crying when they talked about it. I could see that many people were genuinely affected by even the thought of abortion. This made things awkward for my pastor's kid self, who felt nothing.

Ironically, the lack of emotion I had about abortion caused me to feel ashamed and embarrassed. Everyone around me seemed to be greatly moved by the topic. Many of my friends even attended protests outside of abortion clinics where they would wear red pieces of duct tape over their mouths with "LIFE" written across them. I chose to take their word for how evil abortion was, but I really didn't get it.

In the wake of the majority of my childhood Christian friends walking away from their faith, it's pretty clear to me now that many of those I grew up with probably felt the same way I had. The zeal toward revival and the pro-life cause created an environment that silenced the questions and concerns that some of us had. There seemed to be no room for those who were lukewarm, so we all made an effort to stay "hot" on these important subjects (at least by outward appearances).

My problem was that I'd never been able to lie to myself for very long. The realization that I just didn't care that much about revival or abortion steadily ate at my conscience. At some point, I confessed my lack of feelings to my parents. Thankfully, I was met with love and compassion as they reassured me that I was young and there were other things for me to care about in the meantime.

Around the same time, I went to the Lord and told Him something along the lines of "I don't care about abortion, but I know it matters to You. I am going to stop beating myself up about not feeling the way everyone else around me does. Would you please help me feel the way that You do about abortion?"

I felt relieved at the new honesty I had established between me, my parents, and God. Far from being pro-choice, I still found myself generally apathetic about the issue, but I trusted God to help my heart catch up if it really mattered to Him. I still considered myself pro-life politically, but it was more on principle than any sort of heart-felt conviction.

You might disagree, but I am thankful for the way God used those years of apathy to help me develop a strong sense of compassion for women who are passionately pro-choice. I also learned to recognize that it was important to make decisions from a pro-life perspective even if I didn't *feel* moved by the cause.

I heard stories of women who felt they had no other choice than abortion, and my heart ached for them. I could empathize with how difficult it would be to have to choose between your dreams and having a baby that you did not plan for (although now I have a different perspective).

I also could not imagine why anyone would have an issue with abortion in the case of rape, incest, or childhood pregnancy. How could it possibly be God's plan for thirteen-year-old little girls to have to carry the baby of their rapists? How could God desire for severely disabled children who were only suffering to be brought into this world?

My beliefs about abortion colored my views on contraception. Only fundamentalists believed in giving God control over the size of their family. Every married woman should be on birth control so she could choose when to have children. And if a couple was unable to conceive naturally, I was fascinated by the new technology that made IVF (in vitro fertilization) more accessible to the average person.

I share all of this with you to hopefully bridge any gap that might exist between where I now find my views as it relates to abortion and family planning and where you find yourself. If you grew up with a genuine zeal for ending abortion that hasn't changed, I applaud you for maintaining those beliefs through all of life's different seasons! If, like me, you were cynical about the pro-life movement early on and maintained more lukewarm views, or you're pro-choice and always have been, there's absolutely no judgment from me, but I hope to shed some light on a perspective you may not have seen yet.

One of the reasons I care so much about abortion is because our culture's stance on it is communicating something about our value as women to the world around us—specifically that children and our natural desire for fruitfulness are both hindrances to achieving equality with men. We are being told that we need contraceptives, and then abortion when they fail, in order to be viewed as successful.

How devastating that the incredible gift of motherhood and our unique ability to partner with God in bringing new souls to earth is seen as anything other than a miracle. Society as a whole should be supporting women in the role of motherhood rather than seeking a way to "rescue" them. Creating the next generation of human souls is the very core of life because it is the creation of life itself. What could be more significant? What cause could be more worthy than supporting those who maintain our existence?

I see women as the primary creators of culture and the family because we are nurturers, yet I also see a lack of value for WHO and WHAT women genuinely are. We possess perspectives, skill sets, and natural abilities that are simply impossible for men to carry. This perspective is the position I operate from when I think and talk about abortion.

I know that many of my friends have had abortions or have somehow been affected by abortion. I am not here to condemn you. My intention is to hopefully bring light and love and another option to the table. It is clear that regardless of your stance on abortion, it is a "choice" that almost no one wants to find themselves making.

I believe there is room in the pro-life movement for compassion toward mothers who have chosen abortion, for their partners who have encouraged it, and for the individuals who work in the abortion industry. We can do this while prioritizing saving the lives of our preborn children. I am not alone in this stance, as evidenced by the countless organizations that exist purely to help women psychologically after abortion and to help abortion workers find fulfilling work outside of the industry. Numerous organizations raise money, collect supplies, and provide hands-on support for those facing an unplanned and/or crisis pregnancy.

This is another essential preface to some of the more scientific and spiritual arguments I have against abortion. Regardless of these resources, we can definitively say abortion is wrong, but it is still important to note these resources do exist, as a frequent complaint of the abortion lobby is that pro-lifers are only "pro-birth."

The irony of the "pro-choice" perspective is their insistence that pro-life individuals only fight for pregnancies and not for children at every stage of life while denying women who CHOOSE motherhood any real support. I suppose you could say that the pro-choice crowd comes off as not only pro-abortion but also very anti-motherhood—selling the gospel of abortion as a solution to the "problem" of motherhood instead of valuing this important ability that women have to create life.

Abortion has been touted as the saving grace of all women, spreading the message that our motherhood isn't wanted or needed—despite the fact that the majority of women will, at some point, choose motherhood. So, is abortion the ultimate women's right, or does it affirm that our very biology is a hindrance to our societal acceptance?

Being pro-life and pro-choice are not mutually exclusive, depending on which choices are at hand. For instance, we have many choices as women when it comes to our potential for motherhood. We can abstain or use various contraceptives, and if those choices are not an option and we find ourselves incapable of conceiving, we can choose the gift of adoption.

While focusing so intently on fighting for a woman's "right" to choose to abort her baby, society has neglected to advocate for better solutions to a woman's fundamental right to carry a pregnancy in the first place. A staggering percentage of women struggle to get pregnant or maintain a pregnancy (see page 107), and the infertility industry profits.

I have watched countless testimonies from women who have chosen abortion and gone through with the termination or changed their minds at the last minute. What so many of them have in common is that they did NOT feel like they had choices. There wasn't a nationally recognized nonprofit with a multimillion-dollar marketing campaign telling them that they could keep their baby if they wanted and that they would help them be the best mother possible. No, instead there was a multimillion-dollar marketing campaign telling them that their pregnancy would prevent them from accomplishing their dreams, getting an education, or living their "best" life (*ahem* Planned Parenthood). Scaring women into choosing abortion

doesn't sound like a choice to me, and it certainly doesn't sound like the empowering feminist choice that culture makes it out to be.

Women deserve better. Women deserve to have their femininity, their personhood, valued wholly. Women shouldn't have to medically and violently interrupt a natural and beautiful process within their body to be "successful." The modern feminist movement would conclude that any value women lack is due to the patriarchy, but I actually think it's us causing the issue—women acting as gatekeepers of femininity.

As we've discussed, the women's movement was hijacked long ago. First by the sexual revolution and then by the identity politics of the far left—the latter working so effectively AGAINST women that they no longer fight for women at all. Instead of modern feminism working to solve the problems that real women face, they have joined in the oppression Olympics glorified by postmodern philosophy. The more boxes you can check off on the list of victimhood requirements, the more your voice is valued in the women's movement. Lesbian *check*, fat *check*, immigrant *check*, trans *double check*.

The problem is, the "issues" on this imaginary list have little to nothing to do with the unique challenges that real women face. Important topics like advocating for better conditions for working mothers, imposing child support payments on the perpetrators of rape, and more research into the root causes of infertility in women have been swapped with fighting for abortion on demand, allowing trans individuals to compete in women's-only activities, and changing the term "mother" to "birthing person." The absurdity of this narrative calling itself anything other than leftist propaganda, let alone women's "empowerment," is beyond what our culture allows us to recognize.

The rest of this chapter contains some of the scientific and spiritual/moral arguments that changed my mind and then my heart on the issue of abortion. Far from the apathetic position I found myself in for almost a decade, I am now very passionately involved in the pro-life movement. I have found a community that has worked to reconcile the issues with the pro-life movement of my childhood and become more helpful to women. Far from the stereotypical protestors of the early 2000s who dressed as grim reapers outside abortion clinics, today's pro-life leaders are compassionate intellectuals who are seeking to save the lives of the unborn while empowering the women who carry them.

My story is an example of why I think it's super important to understand abortion beyond the religious perspective. Being told that God didn't like abortion wasn't enough to convince me—even at fourteen years old. Maybe it should have been, but I'm sure I'm not the only one who thinks understanding why God doesn't like something is just as important as accepting that He doesn't like it. (This is why we have hearts *and* brains.)

Now that I have an understanding of abortion from a reason-based scientific perspective that is clearly affirmed by Scripture, things are so much more evident to my mind and my heart. I don't just know the facts, but I feel them deeply too—all the while maintaining a compassionate heart toward those who don't have the same understanding that I do. This compassionate position is an important one to start from. Have compassion on yourself for any misguided views you may have held in the past, and compassion on those who have made life-defining decisions that have affected them more than you might ever know.

God did not create an arbitrary list of things and say, "Don't do these things because I am controlling." While obedience to God is hugely important, God also created us with intelligence and the ability to reason. His laws make sense! As we learn more about psychology and science, so many of God's laws have been "validated" beyond blind obedience.

I want to bring balance by also acknowledging that blind obedience to God is something very valuable. First Samuel 15:22 says, "Behold, to obey is better than sacrifice." This type of obedience will be required of most of us at several different points in life because our understanding is not always caught up to His purpose. But hopefully, as we step out and obey beyond our understanding, we seek to learn the why.

Could it be that the Creator of heaven and earth knows the laws of science and our minds better than our technology allows us to comprehend, and seeking out WHY He says things is a noble task? I think so! In 2 Timothy 2:7, Paul encourages his fellow believers to think about what he has said to them and to pursue understanding. We have an opportunity to help people experience the love of God by helping them see the synergy and perfect balance of God's laws and why they work! When we're talking about abortion, understanding beyond "because God said so" can allow non-believers to understand the love and care that God fashioned their bodies with.

Many believers end up not being 100 percent pro-life because they want to define life as the moment a person becomes a person. But there is a difference between life and personhood. We cannot know when a spirit enters a body or when it leaves, but we can know when life begins scientifically. This is why science and theology both matter!

There are big question marks around what exactly defines someone's personhood. For example, when we ask if a brain-dead person is still alive, we don't literally mean alive. If their heart is beating, they are still alive. What we are really asking when we wonder, "Are they alive?"

is, "Are they still a person?" No one argues if a houseplant is alive or not (well, maybe my husband and I after I have forgotten to water ours for a few days), but when we ask if a person is really alive, we are interested in knowing if they have a soul or a spirit.

In Christianity, most of us hold the belief that what animates our bodies and minds beyond simple reflexes and instincts—what differentiates us from animals—is our spirit. This can be understood as the breath of life that God originally breathed into Adam and Eve in the Garden of Eden. As we discussed before, our spirits are mysterious, though very real, things. This is evidenced by the fact that we exist in a dimension that animals and artificial intelligence do not.

Because science has so far been unsuccessful in pinning down what exactly the spirit is, we have to fully rely on Scripture to understand this part of ourselves and what God's purpose in gifting us with it is.

"But it is the spirit in man, the breath of the Almighty, that makes him understand."

—JOB 32:8

"The dust returns to the earth as it was, and the spirit returns to God who gave it."

—ECCLESIASTES 12:7

"The Spirit himself bears witness with our spirit that we are children of God."

—ROMANS 8:16

"The spirit of man is the lamp of the Lord, searching all his innermost parts."

—PROVERBS 20:27

Our spirit was breathed into us by God. It gives us understanding and intelligence. When our physical bodies die, our spirit returns to God. It is a testament to the fact that we are His children. And our spirit searches our depths with the light of the Lord. These are just a few of the things we can learn about the animating spirit that exists in each of us.

Something we don't learn from Scripture, however, is exactly when that spirit enters our physical bodies and when exactly it departs. This might have been less of a concern before medical technology developed to the point of being able to bring people back to life and sustain them for days, months, and even years on life-support. But now the dilemma that frequently arises is, "The machines are keeping them alive, but are they really still with us?"

In pregnancy, it isn't known when our spirit is connected to our developing physical body. I have heard countless theological perspectives on this, including the common Jewish perspective that the spirit enters upon first breath. But in reality, we have no real way of knowing. Through the innovation of ultrasound, we can now watch as our tiny babies breathe amniotic fluid, move, and respond to touch from very early on, but we still don't know if this means these babies have their spirits (or consciousness).

This presents a challenge to many Christians on what exactly to believe about issues like abortion and medically assisted suicide. Unfortunately, most of us have been taught to compartmentalize life as Christians. If the Bible explicitly mentions something, we might apply it. But for issues that the Bible doesn't have a clear answer for, we tend to rely on our own understanding and exclude the Lord from our processing altogether.

As believers, we must have the Holy Spirit integrated into every part of our lives—God is either the King of all aspects of our lives or not at all. By only seeking to include Him on the issues we think are relevant to Him, we make ourselves god and relegate Him to a mere commentator.

Abortion is not specifically talked about in Scripture. We don't have an eleventh commandment that states, "Thou shalt not commit abortion!" But this doesn't mean God didn't give us principles that clearly address issues like abortion and euthanasia. Many modern issues aren't specifically addressed by Scripture, and this is where we must read the Word with the Holy Spirit as our guide on how to apply God's principles to life today.

Psalm 139:13–14 is a reminder that we are each intentionally "knit" together by God in our mother's womb, but it still doesn't answer the question of when His spirit is breathed into us. There is also a lot of debate as to how the psalms should be read and applied to our lives because they are clearly poetic literature and shouldn't necessarily be used to form our views about scientific things.

The Bible might not tell us exactly when we become a person— when our spirit is joined to our body—but it does make it very clear that God takes the shedding of innocent blood very seriously. Scripture also clearly states that murder is wrong and then goes on to define what murder is. As we will get to soon, abortion clearly falls under the category of murder.

I know, this is strong language to use! But remember how we started this section—maintaining compassion toward yourself and others is important in the nitty-gritty of this argument.

Another common theme we see in the Bible is the sanctity of life. Not just human life that is animated by a spirit, but even animal life is given value. God provides guidelines for how to treat animals and even ethical ways to kill them (Deuteronomy 22:10, for example) when they must be sacrificed or eaten. This lends itself to the idea that even if we are unsure if a body has a spirit or not, there is still a requirement to honor its life (we will talk about what it means to be scientifically alive soon).

> "There are six things that the Lord hates,
> seven that are an abomination to him:
> haughty eyes, a lying tongue,
> and hands that shed innocent blood,
> a heart that devises wicked plans,
> feet that make haste to run to evil,
> a false witness who breathes out lies,
> and one who sows discord among brothers."
>
> —PROVERBS 6:16–19

> "Keep far from a false charge, and do not kill the innocent and righteous, for I will not acquit the wicked."
>
> —EXODUS 23:7

> "Whoever sheds the blood of man,
> by man shall his blood be shed,
> for God made man in his own image."
>
> —GENESIS 9:6

> "You shall not murder."
>
> —EXODUS 20:13

The Lord repeatedly makes it clear that children are a blessing and an important part of the Kingdom, further emphasizing the need for caution when we try to use our human understanding to determine when people "become" valuable or not. All life is valuable. Every person, regardless of mental or physical capacity, has a value and a purpose from God, and it is our job as His children to protect the sanctity of life at every stage.

> "Behold, children are a heritage from the Lord,
>   the fruit of the womb a reward.
> Like arrows in the hand of a warrior
>   are the children of one's youth.
> Blessed is the man
>   who fills his quiver with them!
> He shall not be put to shame
>   when he speaks with his enemies in the gate."
>
> —PSALM 127:3–5

PERSONAL BELIEFS AND FREE CHOICE

Now that I've laid out a bit of a framework for the role God and His Word play in the issue of abortion and personhood, let's get into some of the most common arguments in favor of abortion. I hope to provide a spiritual, biblical, and logical counterargument in response to each issue.

I want to start with one of the most common arguments about abortion. An argument that even many who consider themselves pro-life get hung up on. Typically, it goes something like, "I am personally pro-life, but we live in a free country so I think everyone just has to decide for themselves about the issue."

I personally held this belief for years without noticing the hypocrisy in it. This perspective tends to be one that I hear from compassionate Christians who lack a holistic understanding of why this stance is problematic. Their understanding of abortion is typically limited to "God doesn't like it."

Abortion is either morally right or wrong. If it is wrong, then it is wrong for anyone and everyone. If the only problem with abortion was a religious one, it would be against the US Constitution to regulate. As we've already seen, there is actually more clear evidence from a secular perspective that justifies abortion regulation than there is from a scriptural one, although I think it is clear that the right to life is also affirmed by Scripture.

In the United States, one of our first rights is the right to life. This core right is the basis for every other piece of legislation about murder. If you violate someone else's right to life by killing them, outside of cases of self-defense, it is murder. Ending the life of an innocent preborn child, outside of cases protecting the life of a mother, is a violation of the right to life and is therefore murder.

The idea that you can personally be against murder but are okay with other people deciding for themselves if they are is crazy. As a culture, we tend not to view abortion this way because the innocent life that is ended has no one to speak up for it. Unlike most murder cases, where friends and family members speak up and share how devastated they are by the loss of their loved one, abortion violates the fundamental relationship of mother and child. Instead of the child's mother crying out for justice at the loss of innocent life, she is instead made an accessory to her own child's murder.

Is this something we should be okay with others doing? Should we stand by as women are deceived into allowing a doctor to intentionally kill their baby? Do we want to live in a culture that only values and protects some lives?

This is why I find the concept of being personally pro-life but not politically pro-life impossible and selfish. To allow someone to legally choose abortion, even when you know that it is wrong, ends an innocent life, and causes irreparable damage to the psyche of the mother, is wrong—morally and spiritually.

"Reproductive rights' has long been a euphemism for destroying human life in the womb... A phrase that sounds like empowerment is a really only code for the subjugation of preborn children,"

—LILA ROSE

RIGHT TO LIFE

The next big argument is something we have briefly touched on already: abortion in the case of a woman's life being in danger. I view this as a false argument because abortion is never medically necessary to save the life of a mother.[1]

There is no medical situation in which a woman needs an abortion to save her life. Saving a woman's life at the cost of the life of her unborn child is not considered an abortion and is not something that anyone is talking about preventing by law.

There have been some unfortunate ignorant comments from a few pro-lifers that, thanks to the internet, have gone viral. Their views are not the views of the majority of the pro-life movement or the politicians who align themselves with the pro-life perspective. Rest assured that no one wants to place limitations on the right of a mother to have her life saved, even at the cost of her unborn child.

Recently we have seen what are being called Heartbeat Bills passed in several states. This legislation varies a bit by state, but for the most part, it limits abortions after a heartbeat can be detected (somewhere around 5 to 6 weeks).

---

[1]"Dublin Declaration on Maternal Healthcare," September 2012, https://www.dublindeclaration.com/.

On TikTok, we quickly saw stories being shared of women with ectopic pregnancies who were supposedly refused life-saving medical attention by their providers because of the new legislation. Some of these stories were not true, and the few that are demand legal repercussions, because the medical providers failed to carry out their duty to save lives.

Ectopic pregnancies are devastating and scary. They require resolution, either by injection or surgery that ends the life of the unborn baby. This is considered a life-saving treatment and not an abortion because the intention of the procedure is not to kill anyone, but to save a life. Without resolving the ectopic pregnancy, both mother *and* child will likely die. Clearly, saving the life of the mother is a moral decision as well as one that makes sense spiritually and logically. Why lose two lives when we can save at least one of them?

Preeclampsia is another life-threatening condition that women can experience during pregnancy. The solution to this is frequently an early delivery. If the child is born before 21 weeks, they will most likely not survive, but again, this is not the intentional killing of another human, and this child is given the dignity of natural death in the arms of its mother.

Likewise, if a woman is diagnosed with a threatening health condition like cancer, she might need cancer treatments while she is pregnant. These treatments may harm or cause the death of her unborn child, but again, this is not the intentional killing of another human.

If any significant group of people started lobbying to make any of the above illegal, I can promise you that the pro-life community would be outraged. The life of a mother is clearly of extreme importance from a pro-life perspective. She, too, is alive, and most certainly has a spirit living in her body. If saving her causes the loss of her child, it is a devastating outcome, but less devastating than losing mother and child.

I have seen so much misinformation spread about what would happen if all abortions became illegal in the United States. It is simply a lie to claim that there is a significant faction trying to make it illegal or complicated to save the life of a mother at any cost. This lie has been spread by both conservative and liberal voices alike.

Another argument that tends to follow the life-of-the-mother argument is that abortion is the most compassionate choice for disabled children. This perspective is alarming to me as someone who has seen the beauty and life that disabled children can bring to this world firsthand. Ask any family who has a member with Down syndrome if they think their loved one should have been aborted. The resounding response is no!

Should unborn children be killed because they will be in a wheelchair? Should Down syndrome be a death sentence? Is a blind child less worthy of life because they cannot see and will require additional support in life? For most people, it is clear that these are not "valid" reasons to deny someone their right to life, but many people have a difficult time acknowledging that the same right to life exists for children who will have minimal brain activity, painful medical abnormalities, or a condition that will negatively affect the lives of the parents in their role as caregivers.

The idea that only a certain type of person should be born is based on eugenics. Eugenics is the idea that humanity could be intentionally shaped or "evolved" by only allowing the reproduction of people who are considered "desirable." This desirability is always determined by human beings who have proposed many different ways of categorizing people. Some eugenicists have proposed that certain races of people, eye colors, IQ numbers, etc., are inferior.

As you can imagine, eugenics quickly devolves into a terrifying game of god directed by a few people who manipulate science and data to make their case for the destruction of mass swaths of human beings (Hitler was the most famous eugenicist in modern history).

Not only is eugenics clearly very anti-Christian, it is also not based on real science. The survival of the fittest that Charles Darwin explained as the way that most animals, including humans, have developed and "evolved" over time, requires that this survival be determined by nature and not by humans with a god complex. It's not that only the fittest should survive; it's that the ones who survive are the fittest.[2]

Today, the eugenics argument has fallen so far out of favor that the entire structure of its arguments has been rebranded using more "compassionate" language. Instead of claiming that having mentally and physically less-able people is undesirable for human evolution, they will tell you that YOU lack compassion for "forcing" someone who is not born in an ideal body to live. They will tell you that you are cruel for bringing a child into the world who will suffer from chronic seizures, blindness, or some other ailment.

In the recent season of *Love Is Blind*, one of the couples finds themselves in an argument about abortion after the woman says she would abort their child if they determined it had Down syndrome. She claimed it was the "responsible" decision to make because of the burden it would put on the entire family if they brought a mentally handicapped person into the world.

This language is just another way that our culture has justified claiming that only certain types of people are worth sacrificing for. It is a selfish worldview that reduces having children and building a family to building your own ego by having the "best" kind of children possible rather than an act of self-sacrifice and love for other humans—regardless of how deserving they are of that sacrifice.

---

[2] I do not hold a Darwinian view of evolution at all; in fact, the Darwinian evolutionary model has almost completely fallen out of favor with the scientific community.

"Mathematical Challenges to Darwin's Theory of Evolution," Hoover Institution, educational video, June 6, 2019, 57:13, https://www.youtube.com/watch?v=noj4phMT9OE.

Unfortunately, in today's world, medical professionals frequently encourage the abortion of disabled children and present the act of termination as a more compassionate solution. I have listened to the testimonies of many women who found themselves in this situation and chose abortion, and my heart goes out to them. The torment of their decision is evident on their faces and in their words, even as they advocate for pro-choice legislation. Many were convinced by a medical professional who lacked an understanding of the God-ordained dignity of every human life—even those with significant disabilities or deformities.

One of the women shared that she "realized" her desire to continue to carry her severely deformed daughter, who would die within minutes of birth, was selfish. The selfless act was to abort her baby at 21 weeks. If you are unfamiliar with the details of late-term abortion, it is a demise for that child far worse than any natural death. After watching their testimonials, it is clear to me that the burden of having killed their unborn children, terminal or not, had broken the hearts of each of these women in a way that carrying them to full term would not have.[3]

In situations where a child will die within minutes or hours of life, there is inescapable pain and grief, but abortion only adds to the trauma of these moments. It doesn't magically take that pain and suffering away; instead, it exponentially increases the confusion and grief surrounding it all.

JOURNALING:

• Abortion is a topic that immediately brings up a lot of emotions. Have you been impacted by abortion? Take a moment to invite the

---

[3] "What It's Like to Have a Second-Trimester Abortion." YouTube, Vice, 10 July 2019, https://youtu.be/q8-vbOhCqJo. Accessed 12 July 2023.

Holy Spirit to bring healing, wiping away any pain, shame, or trauma surrounding this issue. Know that you have complete forgiveness! If you've been personally affected by abortion, take a moment to check out Rachel's Vineyard. They offer amazing resources to help your heart find peace and forgiveness.

- Let's dive into your personal beliefs and emotions about abortion. Have your views on this issue changed over time? If so, what influenced this shift in perspective?

- Let's talk about compassion. How can we show compassion both to the unborn child and to the women facing difficult decisions? Can we find ways to support alternatives to abortion that prioritize care and support for everyone involved?

- Reflect on the value of every human life, including individuals with disabilities. How do you perceive their dignity and worth? How can we foster inclusivity and support for people with disabilities and their families?

DEEPER DIVE:

- List the four most powerful pro-life points. Give two that are aligned with your beliefs as a Christian and two that are aligned with science/logic.

- Imagine having a dialogue with someone who holds a different perspective on abortion. How would you approach the conversation with empathy, respect, and a genuine desire to understand their viewpoint?

- Consider the implications of not knowing when the spirit enters the body on issues such as abortion and medically assisted suicide. Since we don't know exactly when the spirit enters the body, what should our position be as believers?

SENSITIVE CASES

The final argument I want to cover is probably one of the most sensitive; abortion in the case of rape and/or incest. As I shared earlier, for years I found myself sympathetic toward this subject, likely because of the way this argument is talked about in the media today.

What kind of monster thinks that a twelve-year-old rape victim should be forced to carry to term the spawn of her attacker?

Doesn't leave a lot of room for discussion when it's presented this way. Perhaps another, more helpful, way of confronting this issue is to consider the implications of abortion as critically as we consider the implications of a young girl carrying a pregnancy to term.

Like I said before, we can reason that if abortion is morally wrong then it is always wrong. If someone is murdered, we don't ask ourselves "Well, were they conceived through love, lust, or rape?" as if that has the ability to change the reality that a life was tragically ended. If abortion is murder, it doesn't magically become not murder simply because that child was created under difficult circumstances.

Can we tell a rape victim that she can somehow undo the violence that was perpetrated against her by committing yet another act of violence? Does ending the life of her innocent unborn child do anything other than compound the violence she must go through? Does sentencing the child of a rapist to death absolve the father of his sins?

Far from being an act of mercy for the woman who has been violated in such a violent way, telling her that abortion is somehow a solution ignores everything we know about the consequences of abortion—the death of her child and the mental health crisis that frequently accompanies post-abortive women.

We also know that women who have abortions are significantly more likely to suffer from mental health issues ranging from depression to suicide. This increased risk added to the mental health repercussions of experiencing rape or incestual abuse is not considered enough in the discussion of whether or not abortion is a "compassionate" answer to these situations. I would argue that adding to a woman's mental health issues is not a helpful response.

Something I realized after confronting my own internal hypocrisies as it relates to abortion is that I heard a lot of hypothetical stories about young girls needing abortions after they were raped by a family member, but not very many real stories. I was shocked to learn that rape and incest only make up less than 1 percent of abortions (according to the research arm of Planned Parenthood, the Guttmacher Institute).

If this is the case, why is this fraction of a percent used as a means to justify the entire institution of abortion? I've found that the topic of rape and incest is used as a way to distract from the big-picture argument of whether abortion is right or wrong. By focusing on the extreme minority, we distract ourselves from the majority of abortion cases.

TO BE ALIVE

I know this chapter has been heavy and extensive, but I think it's important to cover one more topic before we move on. What does it mean to be alive scientifically, and what are the implications of that for us as believers?

For some reason, people have no problem understanding what it means to be alive when we talk about searching for life on Mars or the moon. If they were to find so much as a simple bacterium, headlines would read, "Extraterrestrial life found!" Meanwhile, the tiny person being formed in his or her mother's womb gets a "maybe" at best from most people when asked if it's alive.

The body of an embryo or fetus is made up of their own unique cells, distinct from those that make up their mother's body and orchestrated by the careful instructions of their own DNA. From the moment of conception, a new genetic code is created. That code determines the child's gender, eye color, sports proclivity, and almost every other defining characteristic. This genetic code, known as DNA, has never existed in this sequence before and will never exist again. This tiny life is completely unique, and its right to continue should be protected.

In a matter of days, this DNA informs its cells how to organize and form organs, nerves, neurons, and placenta. All of this is orchestrated by this little being, not by the mother or father. The mother's body partners with this miraculous new life to create a hospitable home for it to keep doing its thing. Mother and child then exist for roughly the next ten months in a symbiotic relationship where the mother supplies nutrients for the baby to continue to grow and mature, and the baby provides stem cells that enter the mother's bloodstream and bring healing properties to every part of her body.

This understanding of how life begins means that I have a very unpopular perspective on IVF, which creates countless new lives in the form of embryos and treats them as nothing more than a collection of cells from someone's body rather than the entirety of a new life. IVF can be done in an ethical way, but that is not the way it is typically done.

For believers who are considering going through IVF, I recommend reading the book *Them Before Us* by Katy Faust and Stacy Manning. Christians who are seeking to conceive through IVF must be aware of the many moral dilemmas that exist in the creation of their future children—from how many embryos they create to how they select which embryos to carry, IVF presents a very nuanced set of issues to navigate.

As Americans governed by the Constitution and Declaration of Independence, but more importantly, as believers governed by a sovereign and loving Father, we must fight for the primary rights of human beings. We must fight for life. As Lila Rose, the founder of Live Action, says, we must support every woman in the fullness of her personhood—honoring her God-given ability to mother and nurture.

> "A new commandment I give to you, that you love one another: just as I have loved you, you also are to love one another."
> —JOHN 13:34

> "Beloved, let us love one another, for love is from God, and whoever loves has been born of God and knows God."
> —1 JOHN 4:7

> "Love is patient, love is kind. It does not envy, it does not boast, it is not proud. It does not dishonor others, it is not self-seeking, it is not easily angered, it keeps no record of wrongs. Love does not delight in evil but rejoices with the truth. It always protects, always trusts, always hopes, always perseveres."
> —1 CORINTHIANS 13:4–7 NIV

Abortion is not love. It does not show love to the innocent life it ends, but it also offers no love to the mother. Let us love one another by helping post-abortive women find the emotional support they need, by showing abortion workers the boundless forgiveness of our Father found in Jesus, by refusing to compromise on our stance for the dignity of every human life, and by supporting women in their motherhood rather than justifying the ending of a life.

I finish with this quote from Mother Teresa, who boldly proclaimed the truth about abortion at every chance she had: "Any country that accepts abortion is not teaching its people to love but to use violence to get what they want."

JOURNALING:

- What do you think the cultural implications of abortion have been? What message has the phrase "abortion on demand" given to us about our womanhood?

DEEPER DIVE:

- Take a few minutes to journal about your thoughts on abortion.
- Now, let's distill the essence of your journaling into a powerful declaration of truth. Craft a concise summary that captures your convictions. Here's an example to inspire you: I believe that every human life is sacred and deserving of protection. I am strongly against abortion because it sends the message that the best we can do for women is to help them kill their child, instead of supporting them in their journey of motherhood. I firmly believe in the sanctity of every human life, including those with disabilities. As someone who is pro-woman, I advocate for better resources and support for post-abortive women, women facing crisis pregnancies, and victims of sexual assault. Being a proud Christian, I am inspired by the long-standing contributions of Christians in assisting women facing unexpected or crisis pregnancies. Together, we can foster a culture that values and protects every human life while providing the necessary support for women to make life-affirming choices.
- Let's be prepared to help other women who are in need of support! Get online and find the phone number of your local crisis pregnancy center. Put the contact information into your phone so that you are always ready to help friends and strangers get help in case of a crisis pregnancy. Maybe consider making a donation or volunteering too!

CHAPTER 9

LIVING EMPOWERED

"THE WORD EZER [AS USED IN GENESIS] IN ITSELF DOES NOT CONNOTE AN INFERIOR STATUS. IN FACT, WHEN IT IS NOT REFERRING TO EVE, IT APPEARS SEVENTEEN TIMES IN THE OLD TESTAMENT, AND EACH TIME IT REFERS TO GOD."

—JOHN TEMPLE BRISTOW, *What Paul Really Said About Women*

As we near the end of this book, it's time to analyze how everything we've talked about applies to real life—specifically, YOUR life. In the first chapter, I shared the importance of seeking the narrow path that leads to life. Walking as a woman of God requires a careful balance. The following are some practical ways you can achieve this balance as you embark on walking as an empowered woman of God in the era of modern feminism.

1. Use your empowerment to empower the men in your life.

One of the huge practical ways we can function as empowered women is by using our empowerment to strengthen and set those around us free. In the age of radical feminism, most of us are familiar with the phrase, "Empowered women empower women," which I think, in a sense, is true. But often, this feminist trope is used to imply that if you're truly empowered, you'll also be a feminist.

I recently watched a clip of a sermon from Echo Church in Australia, and the female preacher wore a shirt that I think perfectly sums up what it is that empowered women do. In bright colors, the unexpected message read, "Empowered women empower men." I would expand on this to say empowered women empower men, and empowered men protect and provide for women.

If we are truly empowered, we won't be afraid to empower the men in our lives. Not by having a self-righteous attitude of superiority, but by taking every opportunity to uplift and encourage the men in our lives.

A man who feels believed in and admired by his mother, sister, girlfriend, or wife will almost always seek her out to pinpoint his areas of weakness and needed growth. I don't have any science on this, but I can tell you from personal experience (and the experiences of countless women I interact with online) that this is a fact. A man who knows he is respected, admired, and honored feels safe letting his walls down.

I noticed a night-and-day shift in my marriage when I stopped focusing on all the ways I felt Chris could/should improve and instead focused on affirming him, showing him that I trusted his leadership, and minimized my self-righteous attitude in our interactions. Suddenly, the tender, loving interactions I had been longing for were there!

Empower the men in your life, and I promise you, as long as they aren't abusive or narcissistic, you're going to see a huge payoff. They'll reciprocate by respecting and cherishing you.

2. Dress like a lady.

My next piece of practical advice is to dress like a lady. That's going to mean something a little different to everyone, but the goal is the same.

Dress in a way that accentuates your femininity. God has made it clear in Scripture that this brings Him honor (see page 111). In the era of androgyny that has taken over the West, putting in a tiny bit of effort to add a feminine touch to your daily look is easier and arguably more important than ever. Not only does a feminine appearance bring honor to God, but it also brings honor to your body. As we've discussed before, your body is a physical manifestation of the feminine spirit that God placed into you and all women from the beginning of time.

Part of dressing like a lady also involves preserving your dignity by leaving some mystery. That doesn't mean you need to wear ankle-length skirts or don a burka! It means being intentional about selecting your wardrobe, taking into account the activity, the location, and the people you'll be around.

Modesty has gotten a bad rap in the post-purity culture generation, but I think it's because we've failed to encourage a balanced approach that recognizes the ability to bring dignity to our bodies by how we cover them.

Unlike in the evangelical world I grew up in, in orthodox Jewish culture, the idea of modesty, or *tzniut*, is not about covering the body because it is sexual and, therefore, evil. Instead, the practice of covering the body is intended to honor it as holy and precious, symbolizing when the Spirit of God dwelled in the Holy of Holies. This was a place so honored and holy that it remained covered, and only one priest could enter the space each year after an extensive purification process.

What if we began to treat our bodies in the same way? What if we clothed them beautifully and covered them intentionally to bring dignity and honor to ourselves as incredible creations of God?

For some, this will look like putting more effort into your hair, choosing to get dressed every day instead of staying in pjs (oof, I feel this one for myself), wearing more feminine pieces that flatter your figure, or adjusting how much of your body you will or won't show. There isn't a formula! It's just a process to walk out with the Holy Spirit.

3. Stop listening to Karen.

My next piece of advice is to be constantly vigilant about how Karen, the evil feminist on your shoulder, is affecting your perspective. Question the status quo! There are some feminist perspectives that are so obvious, you'll never fall for them. But there are sneakier ones lurking in the grass, snaking along, waiting for the opportunity to sway you.

One of Karen's biggest tricks that has worked on all political persuasions is the specter of the wage gap. For years we have been told that women are making cents on the dollar for the same work that men are doing. And if that were happening, it really would be a huge problem! The issue is, this "wage gap" has been studied extensively and countless variables and contributing factors have been identified. One of the major contributing factors is that women and men don't pick the same careers. Unsurprisingly, women tend to be drawn to careers in nurturing fields.[1] Careers in teaching, nursing, and childcare are largely overrepresented by women. When men enter these fields, they tend to pursue highly specialized positions, such as anesthesiologists or school administrators. This means they make more money!

When you hear sensational statements like "Women are making less money than men for the same jobs!" simply stop and ask yourself if there might be a reason why. Frequently, there is another explanation besides blatant sexism.

---

[1] Rishi Raj Mukherjee and Shubhank Patel, "A Critical Analysis of the Factors Affecting Gender Pay Gap," *"Gender Sensitive Education: A Necessity to Eradicate Gender Discrimination in India" Journal* (February 2020), https://papers.ssrn.com/sol3/papers.cfm?abstract_id=3635196.

4. Trust God to provide all you need to become who He wants you to be.

When I was thirteen, the story of the child prodigy artist Akiane broke the internet. This young artist, who was the same age as me, was on every major TV show displaying her incredible artwork. Her paintings were surreal works that depicted everything from Jesus as a carpenter to angelic beings in fields of stars.

The most impressive part of her art wasn't even her incredible talent at such a young age but the way in which she learned her craft. Akiane shared that a series of supernatural encounters with God had taught her the intricacies of oil painting with realistic detail.

Unlike the rest of the world, I was very unhappy to hear her story. Why had God chosen her? Why hadn't he chosen me? Was I less worthy of being shown heavenly secrets? I was so jealous of the path God had chosen for her, and I took it as a sign that I had somehow failed God since my relationship with Him was so different. Sadly, a similar mindset still haunts many of us, even as grown women, because we are deeply insecure that we don't have all that we need to live a life that brings honor to God and gives us significance.

This leads to my next piece of advice: Don't allow the lives of other women to cause you to doubt the significant purpose God has for your life. And definitely don't let it keep you from the meaningful friendships he has for you with other women who might intimidate you for one reason or another.

For months, I let Akiane's story miserably fester instead of celebrating God's unique call on her life and trusting that He had good things in store for my life too. If I could only go back to little Justice now and tell her that she didn't need to be a world-famous painter to be worthy of God's love! I've since grown a deep appreciation for the call God placed on Akiane's life while recognizing how many challenges came along with her high calling. Now that I am a married woman with an amazing husband and a baby boy on the way, as a single woman, Akiane could potentially look at my life with the same sense of envy I once regarded hers.

Stop comparing your journey with other women's. Stop allowing jealousy to steal meaningful friendships with amazing women away from you. Remember that God created you with a unique purpose and significance. You've been given everything you need to bring honor to God and live a life of significance. Your story doesn't need to look like anyone else's for it to be meaningful!

5. Swap the Kardashians for Mary.

Another practical way to embrace God's design for you as a woman vs. the world's is to find godly women to emulate. Two great ways to do this are to study women in the Bible and find mentors in real life.

Our culture is obsessed with movie icons, celebrities, and political leaders. Many of these women do have admirable traits worth looking up to, but almost all of them are also pushing values that are the opposite of what God says is valuable. Materialism, gossip, an obsession with youthfulness, and a hyperfixation on career goals don't have anything to do with being a truly empowered woman, yet they are constantly touted by women in the pop-culture spotlight.

Seeking to imitate inspiring biblical women like Mary, the mother of Jesus, can be really encouraging, and emulating her example of a life of surrender to the will of God will bring you far more fulfillment than trying to live the life of your favorite girlboss.

I also recommend seeking out godly women to whom you look up and who can offer you valuable wisdom. For me, this has been my mom, grandmother, aunts, and a few of my mom's close friends. There are other women I look to for specific advice about motherhood, marriage, and health goals. These women have been invaluable in helping me become a more well-rounded and balanced version of myself.

Find those biblical and real-life women who carry aspects of the feminine heart of God that you wish to imitate! If you're struggling to find that community in real life, ask God to help you in your search! I've found so many valuable mentors through Instagram and Facebook groups.

6. Don't leave theology to the boys.

Something practical that I think a lot of women overlook is the need to know Scripture deeply and be able to have intelligent conversations about it. It seems that the fundamentalist crowd has largely left theological exploration to the men, and the progressive Christian crowd has made Scripture reading a literary exercise rather than a source of instruction.

The Bible is the living, breathing Word of God. It's a necessary part of knowing God and our instructions on how to have a relationship with Him, as well as how to honor Him with how we live. That means both men AND women need to know it and study it!

Allowing your husband to provide spiritual leadership in the home is not a reason to disconnect from this incredible gift of God. My husband loves that I know the Bible and have difficult questions that I like to process with him. If your motivation for learning Scripture is to know God in a deeper and more clear way, you can't go wrong! On the other hand, if your motivation is to lord your knowledge over your husband or criticize him for not reading Scripture with the same passion you do, it won't go over very well.

Often, women's Bible studies and Christian books are vanilla at best and, at worst, use out-of-context scripture passages to justify our toxic behaviors. I recommend reading theological writings from different denominations, written by men and women, throughout different times in history. Authors like C. S. Lewis, Alice von Hildebrand, and

Carrie Gress all have beautiful and deep insights into Scripture that will prompt you to ask God deeper questions about His Word.

If there's a particular book of the Bible that really frustrates or confuses you, use that as a motivation to dive in and study it. Read different translations, find different study Bibles or concordances that offer different perspectives, and ask the Holy Spirit to guide you to the truth.

This process of seeking out the hidden treasures of Scripture is a lifelong pursuit, but it should NOT be left to just men—especially not the very small percentage of men who study theology at university.

Thanks to the internet, we have resources at our fingertips that can help us learn about how to properly read Scripture, use study tools, and approach the Bible in the context of its time and place in history. This is a huge blessing that most believers didn't have access to for thousands of years. Don't leave this one to the boys.

7. Protect the sisterhood.

Another way you can be an empowered woman of God is by protecting the sisterhood He's blessed us with. In other words, don't be a toxic friend!

Our culture has normalized gossip and petty behavior between women. I saw way too much of this in the pageant world, and it broke my heart how many beautiful relationships were ruined by it. It is never okay to belittle and talk badly about another woman. It is never okay to talk about another woman's private information behind her back under the guise of "being concerned for her." We are told in 1 Timothy 5:2 to interact with other women in all purity. This means we have to be honest with ourselves about when we're being toxic and straying from the goal of pure interactions. I've done it myself!

And don't try to justify your own petty behavior because someone else is acting even worse—especially as a tactic to avoid feeling guilty.

Even if it's uncomfortable, there is never a wrong time to humble yourself and repent for the ways you've hurt other women in your life.

It's not too hard to make these adjustments with women who think similarly to you, but it can be really challenging with women who are being aggressive and toxic themselves. Turning the other cheek, taking ownership of what you can, even if it's only a small percentage of what the problem is, can provide a breakthrough.

I see many conservative women justify treating radical feminists in a way that is petty and toxic simply because the radical feminists are acting even more aggressive and toxic. Don't fall into this trap. We have an opportunity to break down walls and bring restoration to our sisterhood if we seek to treat every woman we encounter with all purity, especially those who don't deserve it.

8. Focus more on self-development than career development.

Love it or hate it, most of us are getting married later than our parents did, and much later than our grandparents. Feminism has undoubtedly contributed to this trend, as women's priorities have shifted away from building families to building careers. The emasculation of men has also left a huge void of good men who are ready to settle down in their twenties.

Because there are fewer good men available to marry, most of us need to find ways to fill our time while we wait and date. I don't think women should automatically rule out a career as a meaningful way to spend their time in waiting, but they must be careful that the career doesn't become their top priority. When a career becomes your priority, it's difficult to shift your mindset to prioritizing your husband and family later on. Many women will end up keeping their careers once they are married for economic reasons, and in that case, it's helpful to focus on self-development rather than specific career goals. This looks like learning conflict management, gaining project organization skills, and growing your discipline, to name a few possibilities. These are all skills that will not only have a huge benefit to you in your career but also in managing your home as a wife and mother.

In the workplace, unless you're the Steve Jobs type, the harsh reality is that you are completely replaceable. However, your absence at home as a wife and mother has the potential to make or break your entire family—now and for future generations. That makes your role at home far more consequential than the average workplace position.

Don't sacrifice the incredible opportunity to shape the lives and minds of your husband and children by becoming just another cog in the machine. Valuing what God says is valuable and making sacrifices to love your family will give you a deep sense of importance that compares to nothing else in the world.

9. Be a Woman of Faith

You may have noticed by now that I am a person who naturally gravitates to extremes. Whatever it is that I am into, I am 110 percent in. This tendency only seems logical to me. After all, if something is true, shouldn't I live like it's really true?

In 2008, the show *17 Kids and Counting* (which later became *18* and then *19 Kids and Counting*) started playing weekly on TLC, and I was hooked. Here was an entire family who lived out the most extreme form of Christianity I could think of.[2]

The girls in the family all wore long skirts and dresses no matter the activity. "Secular" music and TV shows were nowhere to be found in their home, as any media that didn't fit their very strict beliefs was not allowed. I was especially fascinated by their stance on birth

---

[2]I am not trying to judge the heart or intentions of the Duggars. I am still a fan of many of their family members, but clearly their extremism did not result in perfect children.

control, which helped establish them as one of the largest families in modern history. Jim Bob and Michelle Duggar, the parents of this picture-perfect family, explained that the size of their clan was because God was in control of the number of children they had. Being nine months pregnant with my first has given me even more respect for Michelle, who somehow survived birthing and parenting nineteen children.

It's funny looking back, coming from a very close and God-centered family myself, that I was jealous of the Duggars. I was jealous that I didn't have eight wholesome, skirt-wearing sisters to braid my waist-length hair and share their skirts with me. I wanted my family to go on road trips together to homeschool conventions. I wanted to be sheltered from every dark part of the world around me so that I could make God happy with my good behavior. I looked to the Duggars as an image of near perfection that I could try to emulate. They didn't just talk about their faith; they lived it.

To say that I was shocked and disappointed at the allegations that came to light in 2015 against the Duggars' oldest son, Josh, is an understatement. The whole world was stunned at the revelation that Josh had sexually assaulted a number of his sisters as well as a babysitter in his early teen years. And that was only the beginning. The now-married father was exposed for cheating on his wife with multiple women and, later, for possessing child pornography. The view of the Duggars as America's perfect family was shattered once and for all.

I had a hard time reconciling my fairytale view of this family with the stories of what had been happening behind the scenes. How was it possible for their family to be a symbol of zealous living for God while their own child was stuck in horrible sexual dysfunction?

As Josh Duggar's dark truth began to come to light, similar stories were shared about the hidden realities of other "idyllic" Christian families in America. Clearly, for all their attempts at extreme devotion, human nature still found a way to wreak havoc.

Now, I am not blaming Josh's sexual sins on his parents, but I think that a culture of extremes inevitably breeds more extremes. Extreme sexual repression (for example, the Duggars withholding hugs before marriage) can definitely breed strange sexual preferences that devolve into abuse and child exploitation.

In November 2022, Duggar daughter Jinger Vuolo announced the release of her book, *Becoming Free Indeed,* through an interview with *People* magazine. It was the first time I heard what it was actually like to grow up under the strict rules of the Duggar household. Jinger described how her view of God had become entangled with a sense of confusion about what He wanted from her and a fear of what potentially failing Him could mean for her life and salvation. As I watched a recording of her interview, I was struck by the beautiful place of balance she now finds herself in today. Unlike many who react to previous distorted views of God by throwing Him out altogether, she sought the narrow path of life.

It is a treacherous process to unscramble which of our beliefs about God, His Word, and ourselves are based on truth and which are based on our human proclivity toward extremes. It's easier to react to fundamentalism by refusing to associate with anything resembling organized religion and easier to react to the dysfunctional darkness of the world by diving headfirst into a legalistic relationship with God. My hope is that each of us can avoid succumbing to these inclinations and instead embrace the difficult work of walking the narrow path.

I'm a big fan of clarity. I like to know what's expected of me and have it written in black-and-white language. And while there is a LOT of black and white in Scripture about what God asks of us, there's a lot that is not clear. This can make things confusing if we allow it to. Some people compensate by creating black-and-white where there is none and judgmentally attack those who disagree with their interpretation. Others have written off Scripture as nothing more than a literary work of humans processing "the Divine." I've perceived the Bible both ways at different seasons in my life, but as believers, is it vital that we resist the temptation to resort to extremes.

The Bible was written thousands of years ago in variants of languages that aren't even used today. I believe that it is 100 percent the living and breathing Word of God, and like any living thing, it requires a relationship to understand it and learn how to live with it.

God's Word is His definitive set of instructions for us, and like any set of instructions, knowing the author is the only way to follow them without getting lost in the weeds. Instead of throwing out the whole thing because it feels complicated, we are invited to walk out the messy process of learning to honor and please God hand in hand with Him.

In his epistles, Paul continually criticizes the church communities who think they can create a formula that will earn them righteousness. Instead, he reminds them that righteousness is the undeserved gift that was purchased for us by the death and resurrection of Jesus. Only through faith will we receive righteousness. Our behavior has no bearing on our salvation. Because of what Jesus did, we can get almost everything wrong and still be regarded as righteous. That is a gift that I don't think any of us can fully comprehend.

But the question remains: If faith is all that matters, why are we worried about our behavior and choices in life at all? The simple answer is that when we truly have faith—when we trust that God is who He says He is—we believe His ways of doing things are better than ours. As it says in James 2:17, faith without action is powerless. If our faith, our trust in God, isn't producing a genuine desire to live a life that honors God, it is not real faith.

This is similar to the concept of love within our romantic relationships. If every kind thing and act of service I do for my husband were intended to earn his love, we would have a very dysfunctional relationship. In a healthy relationship, we are motivated to do wonderful things for our partner because of the deep well of love we have for them. This is what God desires with us! He desires us to be so entranced by our love for Him and our faith/trust that we try to do things in a way that pleases Him because of our love for Him, not because we are trying to convince Him that we are worthy of His love.

The popular narrative communicated by pastors and theologians today is that God used to want legalistic observance of His law, but now that Jesus has come, everything has changed. God had a magical revelation that the law wasn't going to work because people just couldn't get it right, so now we have grace. At least, this is the idea that seems to trickle down to your average church attendee. God used to expect one thing, but now He expects another because of Jesus.

I have a problem with this way of viewing God, faith, grace, and the sacrifice of Jesus. The first issue is that we are told that God never changes (Hebrews 13:8, Malachi 3:6, Isaiah 40:8, Numbers 23:19, Psalm 33:11, and many more). This is further confirmed in Romans 3:4, where we're reminded that Abraham was reconciled to God through his faith rather than circumcision. It was because Abraham trusted God and had faith in Him that he chose to physically mark his body with circumcision, not because Abraham needed to be circumcised in order to earn God's good graces. Genesis 15:6 (NASB) says that "Then [Abraham] believed in the Lord; and He credited it to him as righteousness." This sounds a lot like how God works now through Jesus!

If God doesn't change, then why would the things that please Him change? God clearly has always desired us to be reconciled to Him through faith—both before and after the death and resurrection of Jesus. Even the Israelites needed faith in order to live out the Law in a way that pleased God.

During his life on earth, Jesus frequently criticized the religious leaders of his community for emphasizing a walk with God that was based on legalistic observance rather than faith. Again, this was not a new expectation God had for His people, but they missed the message so badly that Jesus had to physically come to earth as a human to demonstrate what a life of faith-motivated obedience looks like.

I would argue that faith is what God was looking for from Adam and Eve in the Garden. After He told them not to eat of the tree of the knowledge of good and evil, they placed their faith in the serpent rather than in what God had told them. It seems that one of the overarching stories of the Bible is God's desire to be connected to His children through their faith/trust in Him as the God of every part of life.

How does this apply to us today? How we live matters. The words we say, the clothes we wear, the way we present the feminine and masculine nature of God, not sinning, etc. All of these things are important! But they aren't how we become righteous or find salvation. Instead, they are the fruit of our righteousness. Just like Abraham, we are reconciled and connected with our heavenly Father by faith. Jesus opened the door for all people to live in faith through His sacrifice! In response, we should naturally desire to live in a way that reflects the family we are now a part of.

What is often subconsciously (or consciously) communicated to us about sin, modesty, and living as women of God is that we need to do these things in order to be right with God. But in fact, when we are right with God, we desire to live by His standards because we trust Him—because we have faith in His ways—not because we need to earn something that we can never earn.

Jesus came and showed us that the law was never meant to be about earning our salvation; rather, it was meant to be an invitation to surrender our plans and our will to the plans and will of our Father. That is the heart of the law vs. the letter of the law that Jesus and Paul both repeatedly speak about in the New Testament. When Israel was focused on trying to nitpick at every little letter of the law, things tended to go very poorly for them. But once Jesus came and perfectly lived the law, we saw that the law was always about submission to the Father.

On our journey toward becoming women of God, it's vital that we seek balance. Not balance according to the world's definition—a half-hearted devotion to God blended carefully with cultural norms—but balance in our approach to living for God.

A perspective on Scripture from Bill Johnson that has always stuck with me is the idea that truth is often held in tension. There are many things in Scripture that people are quick to dismiss as contradictory when in reality, I believe these are examples of the tension of truth. For instance, we are told that God is love, but that is not all that God is. Taking this scripture to its extreme, without balance, leaves us with a hippie God who is unable to exact justice.

While God is love, He is also a consuming fire, and vengeance is His. He is the Prince of Peace who comes to make war with His enemies. These are seemingly contradictory ideas, but they bring balance to our understanding of God. They are facets of Him.

This understanding of Scripture doesn't just exist as it relates to the nature of God; it also relates to what is asked of us as believers in His Word. As we've discussed, faith is where our righteousness comes from, but that doesn't mean we DO nothing. The evidence of our faith is action. There's some of that balance again!

Understanding that God has given us guidelines on how to live successfully as His children must be balanced with the understanding that it is our faith and trust in Him that justifies us, not us getting everything right. Both faith and action/works matter, but those actions must arise out of sincere faith rather than from a desire to earn our right standing with God. Likewise, the way we walk out our femininity, live in fruitfulness, and reflect the feminine image of God must be rooted in a deep sense of trust in who He is. This trust is the fruit of being loved by and loving Him.

There have been seasons where I was "behaving" perfectly but was so burdened by a constant anxiety that I was going to disappoint God that I was miserable. There were other seasons where I was making choices that I absolutely would not make again, but I experienced a level of forgiveness and grace from God that restored my heart and brought me to a place of true repentance. The goal is to live somewhere in the balance of these two approaches—to be so in tune with His kindness and love that we desire to represent Him in our behavior, but rely on His grace in order to do so.

This is what I want to call you, my sister, to do. To walk a balanced life, full of grace, full of faith, imperfectly with Him. It can be tempting to read a book like this and then try to follow it like a law—telling yourself that this must be the formula to becoming a godly and feminine woman. Or perhaps you may feel the exact opposite desire after reading what I have shared in these chapters.

I want to encourage you to think about what we've discovered together on these pages as a beginning and not an ending. Let your questions serve as a catalyst to throw yourself further into the arms of our heavenly Father. Rather than trying to formulate an equation to become the "perfect woman," recognize that we can only become the women of God we are called to be by His grace.

You don't have to be a "girlboss" CEO to be an empowered woman of God. And you also don't have to be a second-class citizen relegated to a life of submission and silence. He is the only one who can help you, who can tell you when to show your power and when to humble yourself, when to display strength and when to boast in your weakness.

Throw off the chains of extremism that both fundamental religiosity and radical feminism have tried to place on us and feel the freedom of God's perfect design, empowering you to be more than you ever dreamed.

JOURNALING:

• Have you ever found yourself drawn to the allure of extremes—the thrill of going all in or taking things to the utmost limit? Reflect on what it was about taking an extreme position that captivated you. How did it influence your beliefs and actions? Did you eventually discover a balance? On the flip side, have you struggled with being wishy-washy? What is something in life you need to take a stance on?

• Let's talk about faith and action. In your own life, how do you make the connection between faith and action? Do you lean more toward one or the other? Take a moment to think about the importance of both faith and action in your spiritual journey. How do they work together?

DEEPER DIVE:

• Share the most impactful aspect of this book on your journey to discover godly womanhood. What has struck a chord deep within your heart?

• As you've journeyed through these pages, have you experienced any shifts in your perspectives? What is something you changed your mind about while reading? Conversely, are there still areas where you hold differing views?

DECLARATION OF WOMANHOOD

As a daughter of God, I declare boldly:
My identity is found solely in Him,
Rejecting the world's influences and distorted religious views.

I am adorned with a sacred femininity, empowered by His design.
I dress to reveal His Spirit, I speak to reveal His Spirit, I live to
reveal His Spirit.

God, You are my Father and I am Your daughter!
I dress, speak, and live to exude Your Spirit,
Acknowledging my flaws, taking ownership of my choices,
Extending abundant grace to my fellow sisters, free from competition.

I repent for seeking approval, striving to earn my salvation,
For despising the beauty of my womanhood, rejecting my femininity.
Now I embrace the fruits of the Spirit, blossoming in Your image.

The Word of God and His Holy Spirit lead me into all truth.
I shake off the shackles that have tried to hold me back as a woman.
I am an image bearer of the feminine spirit of God.

I can honor the masculine spirit of God displayed in men without
feeling threatened.
I empower the men in my life.

I rejoice in my weaknesses, finding strength in my heavenly Father,
Trusting His limitless provision, releasing comparison and envy.

I embrace my unique significance, walking the extraordinary path He
has ordained for me.
I draw inspiration from virtuous women in Scripture and in life,
Emulating the example of Mary and seeking mentors who embody
His heart.

I engage with Scripture, discerning its profound truth through the
Holy Spirit's power.
I embrace my divine fruitfulness, nurturing the souls of others.

God, create in me a haven for the hearts of others to encounter
Your love.
For I am a passionate daughter of God, called to impact the world,
Not by my own power or strength, but by the beauty of Your
design revealed through me.

I am a bold daughter of God,
Empowered to reveal You through my body, mind, and spirit.
I praise You, for I am fearfully and wonderfully made!

ACKNOWLEDGMENTS

I am full of gratitude for the countless people who have helped make this book a reality.

I would first like to thank the Lord for His grace in completing this sometimes-overwhelming task. He used my everyday struggles to help teach me truths that I now have the honor of sharing with you.

To my husband, thank you for believing in my ability to do what I have never done before. You never once questioned if my story was worth sharing and instead constantly reminded me of the importance of sharing the fire that God lit in my heart. My relationship with you has taught me so much about the masculine heart of God and, as a result, the feminine heart as well. Your protection and provision have created a place where I can embrace and explore my femininity. I love you with all of my heart.

Mom and Dad, I could write a whole book thanking you both for how you have poured into me and helped shape me into a woman of God, but for the sake of time, I will simply say thank you. Thank you for trusting the Holy Spirit to be faithful to me from childhood until now. Your constant faith in His ability to parent me has been invaluable in my life.

Mom, you were by my side every step of this book-writing process. You helped me organize my thoughts, challenged me to go deeper, took me out of town and fed me so I could focus on writing, and so much more. You are such a beautiful example of what it looks like to be a surrendered woman of God. How blessed I am to have you as my mother!

My sisters, you have been my best friends from the beginning. You taught me how to have conflict and overcome it. Each of you is so different and has helped me learn to love people deeply, even when they are very different than I am. Grace, you always challenge my thinking in ways that I am so thankful for. Glory, you helped me so much in my organization and branding. Promise, you have really helped me see the nuance in life. You are beautiful and talented and brilliant, and I am honored that God put me into a family with you, Promise, Grace, and Glory.

Amanda P, you have been my longest and most faithful friend. Like a sister, you and I have been through different seasons in our friendship as we have journeyed through different seasons in our walks with God. But through it all, you have been an incredibly devoted and faithful friend. I admire so much about you. You never cease to encourage me in my relationship with God. Much of what I know about friendship I have learned by watching you!

My grandmothers, Grandma and Nan. Grandma Gladys is in eternity now, but her faithfulness to Jesus and continual prayer inevitably shaped me. Nan, I've always admired your poise and hospitality. You have always been an example to me of what a feminine and classy woman should be. The way you have always loved and honored Big Daddy, made your home a shelter of peace for all who enter, dressed like a lady, and sought after God is an inspiration to me. This book wouldn't exist without your influence on our family! I have been shaped by your gentleness and can only hope that someday my future generations will feel the same way about me. I love you!

To my TPUSA ladies (you know who you are!), thank you for surrounding me. You each are examples of humility and confidence in truth. You fight for truth relentlessly but have not become hardened in the process. You know when to be Martha and serve and when to be Mary and sit at the feet of Jesus. I love you all!

A huge thank you to my writing coach, Holly. Thank you for drawing me out and helping me fully develop the things God placed in my heart. You believed in me and affirmed my vision every step of the way. You really went above and beyond and helped me fight for my message! Thank you!

Thank you to everyone at the Fedd Agency for believing in me enough to partner with me on this project!

Marlita, my incredible cover artist, thank you for giving your talent to the Holy Spirit. To be an accomplished and skilled artist is huge, but to then surrender that ability to the Holy Spirit and to use your gift to bless Him is another level. Thank you for believing in what the Lord is doing through this book. Thank you for seeking His guidance in the cover art. I believe many women will encounter His feminine heart for us simply by seeing your art.

And finally, thank you to every person who has believed in me and appreciated my writing over the years. I am just a human who has inevitably gotten many things wrong along the way. Thank you for sticking with me regardless and for allowing God to speak through me into your life. I am truly humbled that you would walk this road with me.